D0225547

# The Temptation of
# the Impossible

# Mario Vargas Llosa

# The Temptation of the Impossible

Victor Hugo and *Les Misérables*

Translated by John King

PRINCETON UNIVERSITY PRESS

PRINCETON AND OXFORD

First published in Spain under the title *La tentación de lo imposible: Victor Hugo y "Los Miserables"*
© Mario Vargas Llosa, 2004

English translation copyright © 2007 by Mario Vargas Llosa

Published by Princeton University Press,
41 William Street, Princeton, New Jersey 08540

In the United Kingdom: Princeton University Press, 3 Market Place,
Woodstock, Oxfordshire OX20 1SY

Library of Congress Cataloging-in-Publication Data
Vargas Llosa, Mario, 1936–
[Tentación de lo imposible. English]
The temptation of the impossible : Victor Hugo and Les misérables /
Mario Vargas Llosa ; translated by John King.
p. cm.
Includes bibliographical references and index.
ISBN-13: 978-0-691-13111-5 (hardcover : alk. paper)
ISBN-10: 0-691-13111-2 (hardcover : alk. paper)
1. Hugo, Victor, 1802–1885. Misérables. I. Title.
PQ2286.V3713 2007
843′.7—dc22        2006036674

British Library Cataloging-in-Publication Data is available

This book has been composed in Janson

Printed on acid-free paper. ∞

press.princeton.edu

Printed in the United States of America

1  3  5  7  9  10  8  6  4  2

For

*Albert Bensoussan,*

the best of translators and the most loyal of friends

The most homicidal and the most terrible passion
that one can inspire in the masses is the
passion for the impossible.

(Lamartine in his essay on *Les Misérables*)

# Contents

*Acknowledgments*                                    xi

*Introduction: Victor Hugo, the Ocean*               1

CHAPTER I. *The Divine Stenographer*                 11

CHAPTER II. *The Dark Vein of Destiny*               34
The Law of Chance or the Order of Coincidence        34
The Irresistible Traps                               41
The Ambush in the Gorbeau Tenement                   43
The Barricade at la Chanvrerie                       45
The Paris Sewers                                     47
Elusive Freedom                                      52

CHAPTER III. *Touchy Monsters*                       56
A Character without Qualities                        57
The Saint                                            61
The Just Man                                         65
A Puritan World                                      70
The Fanatic                                          75
An Angel with a Dirty Face                           80
Collective Characters                                84

CHAPTER IV. *The Great Theater of the World* — 87
Adjectives to Describe the Show — 89
Performance, Beauty, and Life — 92
Light and Shadow — 95
Sets — 96
The Victor at Waterloo — 97
Human Putrefaction — 98
Life as Fiction — 102

CHAPTER V. *Rich, Poor, Leisured, Idle, and Marginal* — 105
Reformist Idealism — 110
The Just — 114
A Society Rebuilt — 118
The Victims: Confinement and Women — 120
A Source of Social Injustice: The Law — 122
A Stupid and Cruel Monster — 124

CHAPTER VI. *Civilized Barbarians* — 131
Long Live Death! — 132
Slow-Motion Progress — 134
Victor Hugo and the Insurrection of 1832 — 138

CHAPTER VII. *From Heaven Above* — 146
The Enumeration of the Infinite — 148
Attempting the Impossible — 154
The Total Novel or the Deicidal Impulse — 156

CHAPTER VIII. *The Temptation of the Impossible* — 165

*Notes* — 179

*Index* — 185

# *Acknowledgments*

I gave an abridged version of this book as a series of lectures at the University of Oxford, in April and May 2004, as the Weidenfeld Visiting Professor in European Comparative Literature. I would like to thank Lord and Lady Weidenfeld; Dr. Nigel Bowles, Acting Principal; and all the Fellows of St. Anne's College, for their hospitality; Professor John King, friend and translator; and all the people whose attendance, questions, and observations made these lectures a most stimulating experience for me.

ticulous of his biographers to date—his biography is, as
yet, unfinished—has calculated that a passionate bibliogra-
pher of the romantic bard, reading fourteen hours a day,
would take twenty years just to read all the books dedicated
to the author of *Les Misérables* that can be found in the
Bibliothèque Nationale in Paris. Because, after Shakespeare,
Victor Hugo has generated across five continents more literary studies, philological analyses, critical editions, biog-
raphies, translations, and adaptations of his work than any
other Western author.

How long would it take the same titanic reader to read
the complete works of Victor Hugo himself, including the
still unedited thousands of letters, notes, papers, and drafts
that can be found in public and private libraries and anti-
quarian collections across half the globe? No less than ten
years, so long as this were his or her obsessive, full-time
occupation in life. The prolific output of this poet and dramatist, the emblematic figure of French romanticism, has
a dizzying effect on anyone attempting to peer into this
bottomless universe. His precociousness was as remarkable
as his capacity for work and the extraordinary facility with
which rhymes, images, antitheses, brilliant phrases, and the
most sonorous affectations flowed from his pen. Before he
was fifteen, he had already written thousands of verses, a
comic opera, the prose melodrama *Inez de Castro*, the draft
of a five-act tragedy (in verse), *Athélie ou les Scandinaves*, the
epic poem *Le Déluge*, and sketched hundreds of drawings.
In a magazine that he edited as an adolescent with his
brothers Abel and Eugène, which appeared for no more
than a year and a half, he published 112 articles and 22
poems. He kept up that delirious pace throughout his long
life—1802–1885—which encompassed almost the whole of
the nineteenth century, and he left for posterity such a

mountain of work that, we can be sure, nobody has read or will ever read it from beginning to end.

One would expect that the life of someone who had generated so many tons of paper scrawled with ink would be that of a hardworking, sedentary monk, confined for all his days and years to his study, never lifting his head from the desk where his tireless hand wore out pens and emptied inkwells. But no, the extraordinary thing is that Victor Hugo did in his life almost as many things as his imagination and his words could conjure up, because he had one of the richest and most adventurous lives of his day. He always embraced everything fully and had an amazing knack of being at the center of important historical events, as a participant or as a privileged witness. His love life alone was so intense and varied that it gives cause for astonishment (and, of course, a certain envy). He was a twenty-year-old virgin when he married Adèle Foucher, but from the wedding night on, he began to make up for lost time. In the many years remaining to him, he performed innumerable amorous feats with democratic impartiality, for he went to bed with ladies from all echelons of society—from marquises to servant women, with a certain preference for the latter in his later years—and his biographers, those *voyeurs*, have discovered that a few weeks before he died, at eighty-three years old, he escaped from his house to make love to an old servant woman of his long-term lover, Juliette Drouet.

He did not just mix with all types of human beings, goaded on as always by a universal curiosity toward everything and everybody. Perhaps the afterlife, transcendence, God concerned him even more than the creatures of this world. We can say in all seriousness that this writer, who had his feet so firmly on the ground, saw himself increas-

ingly as not just a poet, dramatist, narrator, prophet, drafts-
man, and painter, but rather as a theologian, a seer, someone who revealed the mysteries of the afterlife, the most
recondite designs of the Supreme Being, and that his mag-
num opus was not, for him, about the creation and redemption of man, but rather about forgiveness for Satan.
He intended *Les Misérables* to be a religious tract, not an
adventure novel.

His dealings with the afterlife went through a part-
comic, part-horrific period that has yet to be adequately
studied: for two and a half years he conducted séances in
his house in Marine Terrace, Jersey, where he spent part
of his nine years in exile. Apparently he was introduced to
these practices by a Parisian medium, Delphine de Girardin, who spent a few days with the Hugo family in the
Channel Islands. Madame Girardin bought a suitable table—round, with three legs—in St. Hélier, and the first
session was held on 11 September 1853. After a three-
quarters of an hour wait, Leopoldine, a daughter of Victor
Hugo who had drowned, made contact. From that time on,
until December 1854, innumerable séances took place in
Marine Terrace—attended by the poet, his wife, Adèle, his
children Charles and Adèle, friends, and neighbors—in
which Victor Hugo had occasion to converse with Jesus
Christ, Muhammad, Joshua, Luther, Shakespeare, Molière,
Dante, Aristotle, Plato, Galileo, Louis XVI, Isaiah, Napoleon (the elder), and other celebrities. Also with mythical
and biblical animals, like the Lion of Androcles, Balaam's
Ass, and the Dove from Noah's Ark. And abstract beings
like Criticism and the Idea. The latter turned out to be a
vegetarian and showed a passion that would have delighted
the fanatics of the Animal Defence League, to judge by
certain remarks that it made to the spiritualists, through

the medium of the glass and the letters of the alphabet: "Greed is a crime. Liver pâté is a disgrace . . . the death of an animal is as inadmissible as the suicide of a man."

The spirits manifested their presence by making the table legs jump and vibrate. Once the transcendent visitor had been identified, the dialogue began. The spirit replied with faint taps that corresponded to letters of the alphabet (the apparitions spoke only French). Victor Hugo spent hours and hours—sometimes entire nights—transcribing the dialogues. Although some anthologies of these "mediumistic documents" have appeared, there are still many hundreds of unpublished pages that should rightfully appear in the poet's oeuvre, if only because all the spirits with whom he spoke agree completely with his political, religious, and literary convictions, and share his rhetorical self-assurance and stylistic quirks, as well as professing the necessary admiration for him that his egomania demanded.

It is difficult to imagine today the extraordinary popularity that Victor Hugo achieved in his day throughout the Western world and beyond. His precocious talent as a poet made him well known in literary and intellectual circles when he was still in his teens, and later his plays, in particular after the tumultuous opening night of *Hernani*, on 25 February 1830, which marked the symbolic birth of the romantic movement in France, turned the young dramatist into a celebrity, on a par with the fame enjoyed by certain singers and film stars today. His novels, primarily *Notre-Dame de Paris* and, later, *Les Misérables*, increased exponentially the number of his readers, not just in French, but in other languages, where soon Quasimodo or Jean Valjean became as famous as in France. Along with his literary fame, his active political life, as a member of the governing assemblies and as an orator, commentator, and polemicist on issues of current affairs, consolidated his overall prestige, making him a kind of political and moral conscience of his society. In the just over nineteen years of his exile, this image of him as the great patriarch of letters, public morality, and civic life reached legendary proportions. His return to France, on 5 September 1870, with the establishment of the Republic, attracted unprecedented crowds, as thousands of Parisians, many of whom had not read a single line of his work, came to cheer him. This popularity would continue growing apace until the day of his death, when the whole of France, the whole of Europe, wept for him. Paris in almost its entirety turned out to follow his funeral cortège, in a demonstration of affection and solidarity that only very few state figures or political leaders have subsequently managed to enjoy. When he died, in 1883, Victor Hugo had become something more than a great writer: he had become a myth, the personification of the Republic, the symbol of his society and of his century.

Spain and things Spanish played a central role in the mythology of European romanticism, and in the work of Victor Hugo in particular. He learned Spanish when he was nine, before traveling to Spain, in 1811, with his mother and his two brothers, to meet up with his father, one of Joseph Bonaparte's most trusted generals. Three months before the trip, the child had his first classes in a language that he would later sprinkle into his poems and plays, and which appears in the strange ditty that the bohemian Tholomyès sings to his lover, Fantine: "Soy de Badajoz / Amor me llama / Toda mi alma / Es en mis ojos / Porque enseñas / A tus piernas [sic]." (I'm from Badajoz / Love calls me / All my soul / Is in my eyes / Because you show / Your legs.) In Madrid, he spent several months at a boarding school, the Colegio de los Nobles, on Hortenza

Street, which was run by nuns. Victor and Abel were exempted from going to Mass, confession, and communion because their mother, who was a follower of Voltaire, passed them off as Protestants. In that gloomy school, he would later remark, he was cold and hungry and had many fights with his schoolmates. But in those months, he learned things about Spain and the Spanish language that he would carry with him for the rest of his life and which proved very fertile in his imagination. When he returned to France in 1812, he saw a scaffold for the first time, and the image of a man who was about to be garroted, riding backward on a donkey, surrounded by priests and penitents, remained emblazoned on his memory. Shortly afterward, in Vitoria, he saw the crucified remains of a man who had been dismembered, which would cause him to speak with horror, many years later, about the ferocity of the reprisals taken by the French occupying forces against local resistance. It is quite possible that these childhood experiences were at the root of his rejection of the death penalty, which he fought against tirelessly, the only political conviction that he was absolutely faithful to throughout his life.

Spanish not only allowed him to soak up the legends, stories, and myths of a country where he thought he had found the paradise of passions, feelings, adventures, and wild excesses that his fevered imagination dreamed of. It also allowed him to hide from other people the brazen entries that he made in his secret notebooks, not out of exhibitionism, but because of his rather unhealthy obsession with keeping a minute account of all his expenditure. These detailed records now allow us to know, with a precision that is unimaginable in any other writer, how much Victor Hugo earned and spent throughout his life (he died a rich man).

teenth century, that century of the great deicides, like Tolstoy, Dickens, Melville, and Balzac. But he was also vain and precious, and a great deal of the enormous amount that he wrote is today seen as lifeless, as minor literature. (André Breton praised him maliciously, stating that "[h]e was a surrealist when he wasn't *con* [an idiot].") But the nicest definition came from Jean Cocteau: "Victor Hugo was a madman who thought he was Victor Hugo."

In the house on the Place des Vosges where he lived, there is a museum dedicated to his memory. In one of the glass display cases there is an envelope that bears the following address: "Mr. Victor Hugo. The Ocean." And he was so famous that the letter reached him. The word "ocean" also suits him perfectly. For that is what he was: an immense sea, quiet at times and at other times whipped up by ferocious storms, an ocean inhabited by beautiful shoals of dolphins and by dull-colored crustaceans and electric eels, an infinite stretch of choppy waters where the best and the worst—the most beautiful and the ugliest—of human creations live together.

What we most admire in him is the extraordinary ambition of some of his literary works and his absolute conviction that the literature he wrote was not just a work of art, an artistic creation that would enrich his readers spiritually, bathing them in ineffable beauty. He also felt that when they read him, these readers would learn more about life and nature, and would improve both their civic conduct and their awareness of arcane infinity: the afterlife, the immortal soul, God. These ideas might now seem naive: how many readers still believe that literature can revolutionize existence, subvert society, and win us eternal life? But reading *Les Misérables*, becoming immersed in that dizzying swirl that seems to contain the infinite extent and the microscopic detail of an entire world, we cannot but shiver at the intuition of the divine attribute, omniscience.

Are we better or worse for incorporating fiction into our lives, for trying to meld fiction with history? It is difficult to know whether the falsehoods that our imagination conjures up help us to live or contribute to our misfortune by revealing the insuperable gap between reality and dreams, whether they dull our resolve or encourage us to act. Some centuries ago, the novels to which a fifty-year-old man from La Mancha was addicted changed his perception of reality and launched him into the world—a world that he thought was the same as that described in fictions—in search of honor, glory, and adventure, with the outcome that we all know. However, the humiliations, mockery, and misfortunes that Alonso Quijano suffered because of novels have not turned him into a character to be pitied. Quite the reverse, for in his impossible attempt to live fiction, to shape reality in accordance with his fantasy, Cervantes's character is a paradigm of generosity and idealism. Without our going to the extremes of an Alonso Quijano, it is possible that novels can also make us feel dissatisfied with what exists, and give us an appetite for unreality that can influence our lives in many different ways and affect the wider world. If men and women have spent so many centuries writing and reading fiction, it must be for a reason. I know that in that winter of 1950, in my military uniform, shrouded by the drizzle and the fog on top of the cliff at La Perla, thanks to *Les Misérables*, life for me was very much less wretched.

Lima
14 June 2004

# CHAPTER I

# *The Divine Stenographer*

The main character in *Les Misérables* is not Monseigneur
Bienvenu or Jean Valjean, or Fantine, or Gavroche, or
Marius, or Cosette, but the person who invents them and
tells their story, this insolent narrator who is constantly
cropping up between his creation and the reader. This constant, overwhelming presence interrupts the story at every
turn to state his opinions, sometimes in the first person,
always with a loud and melodious voice, and with a name
that he would have us believe corresponds to the real Victor Hugo. He puts in comments about morality, history,
and poetry, he includes intimate memories, he criticizes society and its men and women, with their great plans or
their small misfortunes, and he both rebukes his characters
and praises them. He often assures us that he is simply the
obedient scribe of a story that took place before he wrote
the novel, as true as life itself and as truth itself, that tran-
scends him as a mere intermediary, a mere copier of reality.
What a fairy tale! In fact, he is the astute creator and super-
star-star of this grandiose lie. His creative work is full of
life and is truthful not because it resembles a preexisting

reality, but because it is the result of his fantasy, of the force of his inspiration and the power of his words, of the tricks and magic of his art.

How can we describe this narrator? His most salient features are omniscience, omnipotence, exuberance, visibility, and egomania. He knows everything that happens during the time of the novel, those eighteen years that begin on an October evening in 1815, when the ex-convict Jean Valjean enters the inhospitable town of Digne, and end that night in 1833 when Jean Valjean dies in his small house in the Rue de L'Homme Armé, with Marius and Cosette by his bedside, in the glow of Bishop Myriel's candlesticks. He also knows what has happened before—what the Battle of Waterloo was like, for example, or the history of the convent on the Rue Picpus—and what will happen after the story ends, like urban development in Paris or the moment, far into the future, when the Order of Perpetual Adoration, which sheltered Jean Valjean and Cosette for five years, will go into decline and eventually cease to exist.

He knows everything and he has a compulsive need to tell it all, to display his torrential wisdom, taking whatever time he needs. In few fictions can one see as clearly as in *Les Misérables* the innate desire of the novel to grow, to proliferate, and to endure. The story of the manuscript is that of a progressive enlargement, an inflation of words, characters, and stories. The critics point out that the main difference between the first version, written in Paris between 1845 and 1848—*Les Misères*—and the definitive version, written in exile on Guernsey between 1860 and 1862, is political in that it shows the evolution of Hugo from a constitutional, liberal monarchist to a republican with radical and social-minded leanings. This development can be traced, it is argued, in the changes made in the second version to Marius's political ideas, and the favorable light in which this revised version portrays the rebels who get themselves killed alongside Enjolras on the barricade at La Chanvrerie. In fact, the greatest difference between the two texts lies in their size rather than in their ideology. The revisions that Hugo made to his manuscript were mainly additions and enlargements. What was originally quite a compact story—the story of the ex-convict Jean Valjean who is won over to goodness by the kindness of Bishop Myriel, redeems himself, and scales the moral heights after much suffering—had become, twelve years later, a dense forest. He grafted onto the central story other, independent or related, stories, and many philosophical, social, and religious digressions. This growth is, at times, disproportionate, anarchic. With so many comings and goings, the central thread of the plot sometimes gets lost and the sheer number of commentaries at times strains the attention of the reader. And yet, despite its naive moments and its sentimentality, its old-fashioned effects and its pulp-fiction clumsiness, and precisely because of its torrential force that reflects the frantic pace of life, *Les Misérables* has always seemed to us readers, from the moment it was first published, to be one of the most memorable stories that literature has ever produced.

The axle that supports and spins this excessive narration is the narrator, who is as excessive as the story itself. The ambition of the book is his ambition. He has extraordinary aspirations, and it is through them that these teeming adventures have become so extensive that they appear "real." Of course, they are not real. Quite the opposite. Everything is fiction, starting with what the narrator is at pains to present to us as "history," as a "slice of life," and ending with the narrator himself, the most impetuous invention of the novel, the most complex and most versatile character within it.

Omniscient and exuberant, the narrator is also a narcissist, a born exhibitionist. He cannot stop mentioning himself, quoting himself, reminding us that he is there and that it is he who decides what is told and how it is told. He continually appears in front of the characters, to the point of blotting them out altogether. The ploys he uses to draw attention to himself are legion. The most common of these is false modesty, telling us that he does not want to be there, or that the opinions that we are hearing are those of a character, not his, as when Jean Valjean compares— Genet *avant la lettre*—the prison and the convent, the convicts and the nuns: "Here we exclude any personal theories. We are just the narrator; we adopt the point of view of Jean Valjean and we translate his impressions" (II, VIII, IX, p. 588).[1] It is enough for him to say that for it not to be true; specifying his position is a way of making himself the center of the tale, declaring himself nonexistent is a flagrant way of existing.

On certain occasions, the pretext he uses for making an appearance is his scrupulous precision. Marius and Cosette get married on 16 February. "Now," the narrator says, "we point out this detail for the pure satisfaction of being exact, as it happened the 16th was Mardi Gras" (V, VI, I, p. 1388). (This precision is, furthermore, inexact: in real reality, 16 February of that year was a Saturday.) At other times, he wants to repeat to the reader some pearl of wisdom: "As we have already explained, in a first love, it is the soul that is gripped before the body; later the body comes first and sometimes the soul is not engaged at all" (IV, VIII, VI, p. 1046). In the case of the narrator, the "we" is a sign not of modesty but of pride: he uses the royal we.

The absolute monarch of knowledge, he is conversant with events and their motivations, with longer-term and immediate causes, with the psychological motivation for actions, with the most tortuous meanderings of the spirit, and he often feels the need to suspend his story to remind us of his ubiquitous wisdom.

The biggest mistake that we could make would be to believe him entirely when he talks about himself, especially when he tries to convince us that he is, at best, someone who hears and repeats, a "stenographer": "The two interlocutors seemed preoccupied. We transcribe as exactly as we can the conversation that took place" (II, VIII, III, p. 549). "As we can . . ." We are on to you, you trickster! His stratagems to get himself noticed reach ineffable extremes when, with musical coquetry, he disclaims responsibility for the cacophonies of a sentence by attributing them to one of his creatures: "This sentence, which contains so many 'ofs,' is taken from the report that the prosecutor wrote entirely in his own hand . . ." (I, VIII, III, p. 302).

As well as being omniscient, the narrator is also all-powerful, and one of the ways that he displays this power is by restricting his omniscience on occasion to achieve certain effects, to keep an inconsistency quiet, to cause suspense, or to satisfy his narcissism: to see his own reflection in the text, to talk about himself in what he narrates. In the novel, there are some events that are not completely clear, and this occurs when the narrator decides not to know certain things: "One of the booksellers for whom he worked, Monsieur Magimel, I believe . . ." (III, V, III, p. 702). On this occasion, there is a doubt; on other occasions, his ignorance appears to be complete. When Jean Valjean escapes from the jail at Montreuil-sur-mer, where Javert has imprisoned him, he suddenly appears in his house, at the lodge of the old concierge. How did he manage to get into the courtyard without asking for the *porte cochère* to be opened, the narrator asks. He rejects several hypotheses before concluding: "The point was never clarified" (I, VIII, V, p. 310). These hidden pieces of information are just tactical. In a modern novel, the technique of hiding or suppressing information almost always enlivens the story, adding new levels of interpretation. In *Les Misérables*, the doubts, silences, or ignorance that the narrator owns up to are there to give the reader confidence in him, to persuade us of his reliability as a narrator. He tells us what he knows, what he is not sure of, and what he has no knowledge of. It's he, always he, who has priority over the characters and the story. Like his displays of wisdom, these hidden facts are techniques that are used to increase verisimilitude and win over the reader. In a contemporary novel, this compliance can be obtained only through what is narrated (or, more precisely, through a narrator who is dissolved in the narrative). In *Les Misérables*, by contrast, the reader must give a vote of confidence to the narrator, surrender to his wiles, and accept his overwhelming personality that constantly floods the narrative. The characters in the novel are merely his supports, and the plot is a throne from which he can rule.

That he chooses to restrict his omniscience is made very obvious in the episodes in which the narrator refuses to describe certain things because, he tells us, his principles will not allow him to do so. These eloquent silences reveal the delicacy or the naïveté, the nobility or the prudishness of the narrator. Of all the parentheses in the novel, the most surprising is the one in which he tells us that, despite the fact that the character who is speaking stammers, the narrator is not going to reproduce the stammer because he finds it unpleasant to dwell on another's misfortune: "We mentioned just the once that Toussaint had a stammer, and we ask that we should not have to keep on mentioning this fact. We find the musical notation of an infirmity to be repulsive" (IV, V, III, p. 949). By this stage of the novel, we are already too well acquainted with his likes and his phobias, his fascination with excess and his ability to ridicule a character (like Monsieur Gillenormand, for example) to believe that he is not reproducing old Toussaint's stammer for moral reasons. What is most likely is that the real reason is aesthetic, auditory, that stammering irritates his hearing, which, by contrast, delights in the exoticism of prison slang and is so enamored of antithesis and metaphors. Alongside exhibitionism, the most ardent passion of the narrator is euphonic repetition. He likes to talk, to produce sonorous flourishes, to listen to himself showing off his ability to use language, coloring it, making it musical, molding it into fanciful and sonorous shapes: "Elle était sèche, rêche, revêche, pointue, épineuse, presque venimeuse" (I, V,VIII, p. 187). On another occasion: "Je connais les trucs, les trocs, les trics et les tracs" (II, VIII, VII, p. 575). One further example: "Cet être braille, gouaille, bataille . . ." (III, I, III, p. 593). There are many phrases like these in the book—often written in slang—in which expressiveness and musicality prevail over semantics.

As a conjurer of words, he is quite capable of doing what he says he will not do, and of not doing what he says he will do. According to him, it is not justifiable to describe the morning ablutions of Cosette, because, "in this matter, to contemplate is to profane" (V, I, X, p. 1228). But while explaining to us the reasons why it is taboo to gaze at a virgin's bedroom, he gives a splendid description of the forbidden place and of the rites that are celebrated there.

Something similar happens when Cosette and Marius meet again after the young man's adventures at the barricades of Chanvrerie and in the sewers of Paris: "What took place in this conversation we will not say. There are things that one should not try to describe, the sun is one such thing" (V, V, IV, p. 1366). But in fact their meeting is described with a wealth of detail. Some chapters later, the narrator commits the same offense, when he refers to the couple's marriage: "We shall not take the reader to the Mairie or to the church" (V, VI, I, p. 1389). But he takes us to both places, and, on the way, several events take place. We readers are no longer surprised by these contradictions; for some time now we have accepted the dictatorship of the narrator and have given in quite contentedly to his arbitrary nature and his changes of mood. We dance to his tune, becoming, by turns, sad or happy, depressed or excited, plotters or rebels.

Every novel is a conventional world, and these conventions must be accepted by the reader for the story to have life. In a modern novel these conventions emerge from the narrative subtly and imperceptibly. In *Les Misérables*, the narrator establishes the conventions, communicating them directly to the reader over the heads of his characters, and through gaps in the narrative. "My function includes elements of the priesthood. I replace the magistrates and the priests. I judge, something that judges do not do; I excommunicate, something that the priests have not done." This sentence, found among Victor Hugo's papers, published by Henri Guillemin,[2] defines who the narrator of *Les Misérables* is, and what he does. Judging and excommunicating are, furthermore, pretexts for speaking and Olympian ways of communicating. People who judge and condemn do not listen, they listen to themselves; they have monologues, not dialogues. The narrator of *Les Misérables* is a powerful miracle-worker who reconstructs reality in accordance with his obsessions, through his control over the word, that impetuous, pliable, cadent, chromatic, sculpted speech, whose magical power he is the first to appreciate. He has, in turn, made his characters in his own image and likeness. They also prefer monologue to dialogue; they turn their interlocutors into audiences and the world into an auditorium that listens, attentively and meekly, to monologues that give free rein to the most common feature of this fictive society: wordiness, verbal incontinence. This is one of the main components of the "added element" in the novel, something not drawn from real reality, but rather something that the writer adds to real reality. Like the narrator, the fictive characters are garrulous beings, whose way of communicating with people is not through conversation but through recital, through acting. Characters in *Les Misérables* preach, pass judgment, reminisce, and, if they have to talk to someone, they tend to talk to themselves, like Jean Valjean, who is given the two most dramatic dialogues in the novel: his crisis of conscience over the "affaire Champmathieu" and the confession he makes to Marius that he has escaped the galleys.

Although the characters are very different in terms of education, interests, physique, dress, and social position, they all end up sharing the narrator's propensity for oratory. If one needed to prove how naive it is to measure the realism of a novel by its similarity to real reality, one would only have to ask those critics who see *Les Misérables* as a faithful reflection of reality to listen to the characters carefully, and with a stopwatch in hand. Can we call the extremely lengthy speech that Combeferre delivers on the barricades at La Chanvrerie "realist," when it appears to blot out completely everything around him: the street fighting, the rebels and their opponents, and the whole Faubourg du Temple neighborhood? (V, I, IV, pp. 1207– 1209). And what of the interminable harangue that Jean Valjean delivers to Montparnasse, the young ruffian who tries to steal his wallet in the Parisian darkness? (IV, IV, II, pp. 939–942). Or Grantaire's torrential eloquence in the "Cabaret Corinthe"? (IV, XII, II, pp. 1114–1118). Why does no one interrupt them, gag them, or tell them to stop? Because even though in fictive reality, many laws are violated, the law that everyone adheres to is to let others speak so that they themselves can later speak at leisure. This is the reason why, curiously, in a society of such talkative people, we have the feeling that they are not talking to each other, that communication is poor. The world of *Les Misérables* is one of people confined within their speeches, beings whose oratorical frenzy has made them solipsistic.

The supreme example of garrulous lack of communication is Marius's grandfather. Although Gavroche displays a streetwise, tender, picaresque humor, the main comic character in the novel is Monsieur Gillenormand, the bourgeois monarchist, the visceral reactionary, the inflexible snob, the pathetic, dotty grandfather. Although when he first appears, we hear him exchanging some words with his family, after his split with Marius, he communicates in long, spluttering monologues, in an attempt to drain off the river of words that are drowning him. Whether he is suffering or happy, his speeches are never far from being farcical, and his entrances and exits are the most histrionic in this eminently theatrical world. The funniest of these is, without doubt, when he chokes back the name of the guillotined monarchist poet André Chénier so as not to offend the republican sympathies of his grandson, but finally shouts it out later to a startled Basque (V, V, III, pp. 1366). All of

Gillenormand's monologues were greatly enlarged in the 1860–1862 version, to the extent that the grandfather's speech at the wedding of Marius and Cosette is four times as long as in *Les Misères* (V, VI, II, pp. 1401–1405). These excesses cannot be explained merely by the comic possibilities that this farcical figure, Monsieur Gillenormand, offers the narrator. His comic foibles are, deep down, something very serious. They express an important aspect of fictive society: the conventions, the established fashions, and the clichés of a social class. His sayings, expressions, judgments, and prejudices establish a "rhetorical level" in the novel. Here, it is not a question of what the characters believe, feel, love, or hate, but rather what it is deemed tasteful to say about these feelings or beliefs in the salons, on the rostrum, on walks along the Boulevard, or in the text of a letter. These intellectual, moral, political, and aesthetic standards have been imposed formally—rhetorically—on society by the class that has the power to impose them. These standards are rhetorical, conventional, and in practice no one fully complies with them. Monsieur Gillenormand does not seem to realize that there is a huge gap between theory and practice, between rhetoric and life, and this makes him the most amusing of all the characters; also the least real character within the unreality of the fiction.

The discursive nature of the narrator brings another "added element" to *Les Misérables*: its gentle pace, the slowness of time. The description of the eighteen years covered by the story is very slow. At times it seems that this weary time has stopped flowing altogether, that fictive reality has become a world without chronology, a pure, immobile, space. This impression is particularly strong in what I like to refer to as the "volcanic craters" in the novel, which are the most intense and concentrated episodes, like the ambush at the Gorbeau tenement, the barricade at La Chanvrerie, or the meeting in the Paris sewers of Javert, Thénardier, Jean Valjean, and Marius. The narrator makes these scenes longer and longer, keeping them in focus, spinning them out in an eddy of words. Readers today, who are used to the tightly structured, short, rapid novels of our times, in which there are many facts hidden, and in which the narrator narrates as much by omission as by commission, might feel impatient at this slowness. Usually in a modern novel, except when there are narrator-characters, the narrator is a hidden fact, an absence, something implied. In *Les Misérables*, this is not the case. Although he is the most prominent character in the novel, he is not an integral part of the story, despite the fact that he takes every opportunity to show off in the midst of his protagonists. This is one of the reasons for the slow pace of the story.

And yet, were it not for this great number of words, the novel would not be as powerful as it is. In the middle of correcting the proofs, Albert Lacroix, the bold young Belgian publisher who had managed to persuade Hugo to give him the manuscript, became alarmed at its length and dared to suggest that certain "philosophical parts" might be cut. Hugo curtly refused: "Quick, light drama would have a twelve-month success; deep-felt drama will be successful for twelve years," he replied. He underestimated the success. Although while we are reading, we might find the length of some episodes exasperating, without these *longueurs*, the novel would not communicate to us its "deep-felt drama," would not give us the impression that it is a complete world, a reality described in its totality.

Totality is a key word to describe the novel. For the novel, in some innate, intrinsic way, aspires to totality, and it mixes the quantitative with the qualitative in a curious dialectic. The intensity of a narrative world, its psychological richness, its intellectual and social complexity also depend on something that is very difficult to determine, the question of length. Quantity is one of the ingredients in the quality of a novel. In *Les Misérables*, the naïveté of its moral and social philosophy, the melodramatic nature of many of its episodes, and the psychological simplicity of some of its characters would make it difficult for readers to accept its "reality" if, in the course of the extended, parsimonious development of the story, they did not end up realizing that all this is happening not in our world, but "out there," in the world of fiction. It is a world that is less complex, unpredictable, and evasive than real reality, but one that is equally extensive, numerous, and diverse. The ways in which its rules, rites, habits, ways of feeling, and modes of expression are combined can, through their internal logic and the sweeping, powerful way they are expressed, persuade the readers of the "truth" of this world.

The novel would not be able to communicate this illusion if the narrator were not able to convince the reader that he is telling them *everything*: "Since this is the story of many people of our time, we think it useful to follow all the phases, step by step, and point them all out" (III, III, VI, p. 645). The narrator follows this dictum faithfully, describing events with a wealth of detail and adding his own reflections on what he is narrating, whom he is talking to, and how he is narrating. What holds this mass of information, ideas, images, facts, theories, and morals together is not the novel's plot or its characters: it is the narrator.

Let me give some examples of this narrative slowness. Gavroche is taking the two defenseless little children whom he has found in the street (who are his brothers) to the Elephant of the Bastille, and the story stops for the narrator to speak: "Please allow us to stop here and point out that we are dealing with simple reality . . ." This parenthesis reminds the reader instead that we are not in the world of reality, of fact, but of fiction, that between that world and the novel there is an unbridgeable gap. The narrator then states that twenty years earlier, the magistrates in Paris had tried the case of a child who had been found sleeping inside the Elephant of the Bastille, which Gavroche now uses as a shelter. And after offering this proof of the "reality" of his story, he closes the parenthesis with a bow: "Having verified this fact, let us proceed" (IV, VI, II, p. 976). He tells the story, he has the proof, and he shows us the proof. He is the trunk that supports the leafy branches of the story, the flowering of characters and ideas. He invents and establishes all the links in this complex world. In the middle of the revolutionary struggle in the Faubourg du Temple, the action stops and the narrator leads us to a haven of peace, in the Luxembourg Gardens. Why does he cut off one of the most absorbing events in this way? He is already there ahead of us, giving his reasons: "For the gaze of the dramatist must be present everywhere" (V, I, XVI, p. 1242). In a slightly earlier description of the barricade, he makes another first-person intervention to let us know that he was there as well: "I remember a butterfly fluttering up and down the street. Summer does not abdicate" (V, I, I, p. 1199).

These parentheses that allow the narrator to talk about things that concern him, rather than the story, become a defining aspect of the fictive reality, one of its main characteristics, like the way that its inhabitants suffer from the vice of oratory, and that time passes in spurts or is subject to long periods of immobility. The torrential narrator scarcely lets the readers make their own guesses, have their own intuitions, because he fills in all the blanks: he says *everything*. The description of the convent of Petit-Picpus gives him the pretext to recount the whole history of the order and allows him to promulgate his heterodox theories on religion and faith—against organized prayer and in favor of individual prayer, against religions and in favor of "religion," against the Church, and in favor of God—and none of this would have anything to do with the novel if he, the common denominator, the source of the story, were not there to tell us that the long digression "completes the general picture of the convent in the mind of the reader" (II, VI, V, p. 512). A few pages later, there is another typical interruption: "At this point in our story, it is useful to explore the physiology of Fauchelevent" (II, VIII, I, p. 452).

The narrator tells us the story and his story, tells us what is happening and what the reader must deduce is happening. It is in this dense combination of different elements— what belongs to the narrator and what belongs to the narrative—that the novel is at its most subtle and complex. As a result of this diffuse mixture, the novel has an ambiguity that history itself does not have. On repeated occasions, the narrator assures us that he is telling the truth, that the novel is a scrupulous portrait of real experience: "The events that are to be related belong to a dramatic and living reality which historians sometimes neglect owing to lack of time and space. Yet we must insist that it is here that we find life, palpitation, and human tremor. Small details, I think we have already said, are like the foliage of great events . . ." (IV, X, II, p. 1081).

These are grand and elegant words, and there is no doubt that the narrator believes them. We cannot believe them. The events that he recounts are not the truth, nor are they real life or history. They are "the truth," "the life," and "the history" of the novel: of a lie. But the narrator has achieved something more daring than he had intended. His is not a faithful portrait, but rather a re-creation of life that is as unfaithful as it is creative. It is not a reproduction of reality, but a transgression of reality that we accept through its power of persuasion. It is not life itself, but the disturbing illusion of life that successful novels convey. It is a radical lie, which is the truth of good literature, through which true life is made more comprehensible and more ambiguous, sometimes more bearable and sometimes more unbearable.

Who is this narrator? He is convinced that he is Victor Hugo himself and that we should believe the same. This double belief explains the naturalness with which he shares with us so many personal matters, making us privy to the nostalgic moments and intimate memories that assail him while he is narrating. We have seen how he introduces himself in person when he remembers that "white butterfly" fluttering in the middle of the Paris insurrection of 5 June 1832. The flesh-and-blood Victor Hugo did, indeed, find himself on the streets when the revolt began. On another occasion, there is a new, personal reference to that event: "An observer, a dreamer, the author of this book, who had gone to see the volcano up close, found himself in the passage caught in a cross fire. There with nothing but the half-pillars separating the shops to protect him from the bullets; he was caught in this delicate situation for nearly half an hour" (IV, X, IV, p. 1090). In other chapters he makes one of his typical switches—from third to first person—to continue, as Victor Hugo, a discussion that he had had with Gérard de Nerval about the existence of God (" 'Perhaps God is dead,' Gérard de Nerval said one day to the writer of these lines, confusing progress with God and believing that the interruption of movement signifies the death of the Supreme Being," V, I, XX, p. 1260), or to evoke, in a melancholic way, the strolls that he took around the outskirts of the city when he was "an explorer of the environs of Paris" ("le rôdeur de barrières," III, I, V, p. 595). The beginning of book 5 of part 2, "The Twists and Turns of Strategy," is an extensive commentary on his exile and on the transformations that took place in Paris in the years that he was away, to such an extent that what he is about to describe, he feels, no longer corresponds to reality: "Allow him therefore to speak of that Paris as if it still existed" (II, V, I, p. 462).

These personal interventions in many cases correspond to Victor Hugo's life, as do the allusions to his surname and his family. "He was in the cemetery at Eylau where the heroic Captain Louis Hugo, uncle of the author of this book . . ." (III, III, II, pp. 628–629); "Memories, affectionate and respectful, since they concern his mother (the narrator's mother)" (III, III, IV, p. 639). There are also references to earlier novels. He assures us that he was the first person to use the word *gamin* in *Claude Gueux* (III, I, VIII, p. 599), a claim that critics dispute, and that thirty years earlier, he had been ahead of Balzac and Eugène Sue in having his characters talk in slang in his novel *Dernier Jour d'un condamné* (IV, VII, I, p. 1002). There is even a reference to Hugo's play *Hernani*, when Monsieur Gillenormand repeats the criticism that the most conservative bourgeois circles delivered when it was first staged (III, V, V1, p. 711).

Other affirmations are less easy to prove, whether he is referring to the landscape ("The writer of these lines, digging in the loose earth of that hillock, found . . . ," III, I,

VII, p. 336), or referring to documents that, he assures us, he has consulted, to demonstrate the veracity of what he is narrating ("In 1848, the author of this book had in his hands the special report on this episode delivered to the Prefect of Police in 1832," IV, XII, VIII, p. 1141). Let's give him the benefit of the doubt and accept that the events and personal opinions threaded through the narrative are trustworthy, and that this narrator—who steps magnificently out of the story in "The Entrails of the Leviathan" to pontificate on the excellence of human excrement as a fertilizer, to deplore how Paris wastes this potential fertilizer, and to involve us in his argument ("Feel free to waste this richness and if you want, you can even laugh at me: that will show the extent of your ignorance!" V, X, I, p. 1282)—always tells the truth when he is mentioning autobiographical details.

Is this enough, then, for us to conclude that the narrator of *Les Misérables* and Victor Hugo are the same person? Of course not. He is a character who is usurping an identity, just as the episodes of the novel claim to have occurred in reality when, in truth, they exist only in fiction. Like his characters, the narrator is a simulacrum, an imaginary and remote transformation of the Victor Hugo who wrote masterpieces, summoned spirits on moving tables, made passes at his female servants, and corresponded with half the world. In the same way, Monseigneur Bienvenu Myriel and Jean Valjean in the novel are transformations of Bishop Miollis de Digne and the questionable galley slave Pierre Maurin, on whom their characters might have been based. However many "truths" we can find among the things that he says, it is obvious that he pens infinitely more "falsehoods," and that his testimonies could never rival his fantasies and inventions. Even though historical material plays a central role in *Les Misérables*—and I am referring not only to the great events like Waterloo or the insurrection of 5 June 1832, but also to the range of real people and stories that he used—the fictive ingredients are infinitely more numerous, and the simple fact that they coexist and become fused in the book indicates that the whole novel is a work of imagination. It is enough for there to be one ghost in a meeting for everyone present to acquire a ghostly air; one miracle is enough for the whole world to become miraculous.

The narrator of a novel is never the author even though he might take his name and use his biography. If the novel is a novel—a book in which the truth of what is narrated depends not on its fidelity to something preexisting, but on its own power of persuasion, on its words and its imagination—then these pieces of information will inevitably become transformed into fictional material when they combine with other material that has been dreamed, invented, or stolen by the author from sources other than that of reality, when they become disembodied and turn into words, music, image, order, rhythm, narrative time. In a novel, the author's first invention is always the narrator, be it an impersonal narrator, who narrates in the third person, or a narrator-character, who is part of the action, who narrates in the first person. This character is always the most difficult to create because the truth or the falsehood, the richness or the poverty of what is narrated will depend on how this master of ceremonies leaves or enters the story, the place and time that he chooses for the narrative, the level of reality that he chooses to recount an incident, the information that he offers or hides, and the time that he dedicates to each character, event, or place.

The narrator is never the author, because the author is free while the narrator acts within the rules and limits laid down by the author. The author can choose, with enviable freedom, the form of the rules. Narrators are free only to move in accordance with the rules, and their very existence is constituted by these rules made language. The author's reality is the infinite domain of human experience, the reality of the senses, of actions, dreams, knowledge, and passions. The narrator's reality is limited by the two tools that he has at his disposal to give the fiction an appearance of reality: words and the order of the narration. All novelists invent narrators, bestowing on them a particular way of being and precise faculties and limitations, which are dependent on what they are required to narrate. This task—to invent someone to narrate what one wants to narrate—is the most important thing a novelist does, and yet, until relatively recently, novelists did not even know this to be the case, and, like Victor Hugo writing *Les Misérables*, they did it intuitively or mechanically.

If one thing distinguishes the classical novelist from the modern novelist, it is precisely the problem of the narrator. The awareness or lack of awareness with which they tackle and resolve this problem establishes the cutoff point between the classical and the contemporary novelist. In French narrative it is possible to give a title, a name, and a date to this cutoff point, although, of course, this does not mean that, from that time onward, all novels would be modern. There are still antiquated novels being written without their authors' realizing it (precisely because they do not realize it).

Although *Madame Bovary* was published six years before *Les Misérables*, one can say that the latter is the last great classical novel, while the former is the first great modern novel. With *Madame Bovary*, Flaubert inaugurated a narrative form that would revolutionize the novel. He killed off the innocence of the narrator and introduced a self-consciousness or guilty conscience in the teller of the story, introducing the idea that narrators must "abolish themselves" or justify themselves artistically. Flaubert was the first novelist to pose the presence of the narrator as a central problem in the novel's structure, the first to realize that the narrator was not the author but the most ambiguous character that the author of a novel creates. He made his narrators impersonal, invisible, a technique that, since then, most novelists have followed. Making these narrators invisible means not excising them, but rather making them astute, calculating, and deceitful: disseminating them throughout the narrative. Of course, since Flaubert there have been many novelists who, like the classical writers, narrate through narrators who are not conscious of themselves, who believe themselves at times to be God, at other times the author. These narrators can split themselves—sometimes into the person who is narrating, sometimes into the person who is writing—jumping merrily from first to third person and back again to first person without even noticing. Thanks to Flaubert, these novelists are born old, and the reader of these novels, who might know nothing about narrative form, feels that they are old-fashioned, that they are not persuasive. The conventions have changed, and readers who are now accustomed, through the modern novel, to narrators who are conscious of themselves, who take themselves out of, or put themselves into, the narrative according to rules that are as precise and inflexible as those governing the characters, feel—when faced with these old-style conventions—what the readers of the first modern novels must have felt initially: a certain disorientation giving way to skepticism.

With *Les Misérables*, the narrator reaches the pinnacle of unconsciousness, as if he had somehow guessed that the magnificent spectacle that he is giving us is his swan song, that his days are numbered. There he is, legislating, thundering on, authoritarian, shameless, certain that he has the same absolute control over the reader as he has over his characters, convinced that whoever listens to him, or reads him, believes religiously in what he is saying because of his inspiring nature, the beauty of his words, and the passion of his arguments. In fact, this puppet-master is giving his final performance. Those who come after him will not let themselves be seen by the public, will hide the strings that move their dolls, so that the reader will think not that the characters of the novel are puppets, who live on borrowed, extremely ordered, time, but rather that they are free beings, in control of their actions and responsible for their decisions. This freedom of the characters is contagious. The reader of a modern novel also feels free when reading the story, free to understand what is happening, and to interpret what the characters are doing or are no longer doing, to imagine what they will do, and to fill in the hidden pieces of information. When these readers who have been educated by modern narrative conventions read a classic novel, with a narrator who brutally reminds them that this freedom does not exist, that everything is a game, that the story will not develop through the active participation of the reader, but that it is already there, worked out to the smallest detail, then they must reappraise their reading expectations, reeducate themselves, become used to narrative conventions that will be at first disconcerting, just as their great-grandparents were disconcerted by the first modern novels.

Perhaps this is one of the reasons why many people have the impression, which is totally false, that *Les Misérables* is a novel for children. Its author did not consider it such, nor did the enormous numbers of readers in the nineteenth century who read it with an enthusiasm that very few books in history have stirred up. It was not considered a children's book by Tolstoy, who called it "the greatest of all novels"—it is often said that the novel was very influential in Tolstoy's conception of *War and Peace*—or by Baudelaire, who, after praising it in one of his intelligent articles, called it, in a letter to his mother, "a disgusting and inept novel," or by the anarchist P. J. Proudhon, who thought that "with works like this, one can poison a nation," or by those who considered it subversive, like Narciso Gay of the Royal Academy of the Arts in Barcelona who, scarcely a year after the appearance of *Les Misérables*, wrote a lengthy study condemning it as "[a]n immoral novel, a socialist novel, an anarchist novel, a tremendous, defamatory libel against society."[3]

It is nothing of the sort, nor is it a testimonial account of French society between 1815 and 1833, but rather a splendid fiction, invented out of that reality and out of the ideals, dreams, traumas, anguish, obsessions—the demons—of France's first romantic. The documentary aspects of the novel are not very exact and have aged. What still retains its freshness and enchantment is everything that Victor Hugo stylized, everything that his imagination embellished. Even though it is unreal, it expresses a profound truth: the truth of certain dreams, fears, or desires of ours that chime with the dreams, fears, and desires that he brought to life in his magnificent invention.

CHAPTER II

# The Dark Vein of Destiny

It is often the case that in a world like that portrayed in *Les Misérables*, governed, as we have seen, by a narrator with such an overbearing manner, life seems determined by a force superior to the individual characters, and to society itself, a force that hides behind hazy terms like "destiny," "chance," "coincidence," "fate." In a sentence that was not in *Les Misères*, the divine stenographer lectures us on an inexorable law: "Do what we may to shape the mysterious block out of which our life is quarried, the dark vein of our destiny will always show forth within it" (I, VI, I, p. 212). To explore the manifestations of this dark vein in the novel is the best way of finding out what life is like in the fictional reality, what freedom human beings enjoy there, and what other factors determine their happiness or unhappiness.

## The Law of Chance or the Order of Coincidence

The sheer abundance of episodes and characters in the novel can be disconcerting at times, giving an impression of disorder. But this is a superficial impression because, beneath the effervescent plot, an invisible and inflexible structure links the innumerable events and organizes the disparate throng. This secret order is part of that "added element" that makes fiction independent of the real world.

In *Les Misérables*, chance is not what its name seems to indicate, an accident, something unforeseen and exceptional, a break with normality, but it is something constant that continually affects the lives of the characters, molding them and driving them toward happiness or unhappiness. The narrator talks of "these mysterious workings of chance that occur so frequently" (III, III, VIII, p. 656). In fictive reality only the observation about "frequency" is correct because, once the reader becomes familiar with the environment in which Jean Valjean lives, these workings are no longer mysterious and become instead manifestations of the law that gives rhythm and fluidity to life.

Fortuitous meetings, extraordinary coincidences, intuitions, and supernatural predictions, an instinct that, beyond reason, drives men and women forward, toward good or evil and, in addition, an innate predisposition that puts society on the road to progress and inclines men and women toward virtue, these are all the essential characteristics of this world. In this world, curiously, we find at play both the simple determinism of the romantic *feuilleton* and a complex analysis of the eternal dilemma between chance and necessity or, in other words, an analysis of human responsibility for individual destinies.

The narrator defines the novel as a "play whose pivot is a social outcast, and whose real title is *Progress*." And he adds: "The book that the reader now contemplates, charts, from start to finish, as a whole and in all its details, despite the gaps, exceptions, or weaknesses it may contain, the advance from evil to good, from injustice to justice, from falsity to truth, from night to day, from appetite to conscience, from putrefaction to life, from bestiality to duty, from hell to heaven, from nothingness to God. The starting point: matter; the point of arrival: the soul. The hydra at the beginning and the angel at the end" (V, I, XX, pp. 1266–1267).

Put like that, it appears simple, but it is not, because, on the one hand, in this "advance from evil to good" there are so many "exceptions and weaknesses" that the ultimate objective seems to vanish like a mirage. On the other hand, it is only in the case of Jean Valjean that this spiritual purification can be said to be absolute (although, as we shall see, this assertion can also be countered). The same is not true of other characters, and there is no guarantee at all that most of society will experience a similar conversion, or that they will, as a group, acquire, like the ex-convict, high moral standards. The narrator's optimistic vision in *Les Misérables* is certainly qualified, and, on occasion, contradicted, by the events of the novel.

What the reader is often confronted with in this fiction are the happy coincidences that, at the turn of every page, complicate the story, increase the suspense, and add greater emotional weight to the drama. There is a law of chance, a complicit fate, according to which things always happen in a way that best suits the action, so that it has to be old Fauchelevent, one of the few inhabitants of Montreuil-sur-mer to bear a grudge against Monsieur Madeleine, who falls and is caught between the wheels of a cart, in order that Madeleine can save him (I, V, VI, pp. 181–184).

The scene where old Fauchelevent is saved shows how paradoxical this law of chance can be. Despite the fact that there are a number of onlookers at the scene, watching the old man gradually being crushed by the weight of the sinking cart, and that they have sent for a jack to lift the cart, no one thinks that if they all lend a hand and work together, they will be able to rescue the old man from the trap. They all seem to be tacitly convinced that the old man must be rescued by just one person. When Jean Valjean offers a reward of twenty louis d'or for *one* man to try to lift the cart, nobody takes him up. Why? Because the plot requires that Valjean himself must lift the cart alone, to illustrate his goodness and his strength and to make Fauchelevent morally indebted to him, a debt that the old man will later repay when he shelters the ex-convict and Cosette in Petit Picpus.

Is it not a remarkable coincidence that one of the "friends of the ABC Society"—Laigle de Meaux—should be in the Law Faculty when Professor Blondeau was calling the roll and had the presence of mind to say "Present" when Blondeau called out Marius's name, which saved him from being expelled? Is it not also remarkable that Laigle de Meaux himself should happen to be in the doorway of a café in the Latin Quarter just as Marius was passing in a cab and that he would recognize Marius, whom he had never seen, from a card attached to his traveling bag? (III, IV, II, pp. 674–677). This happens precisely at the moment when Marius has left his grandfather's house and has nowhere to go. These coincidences put the young man in contact with Courfeyrac and the other insurrectionists, and allow the novel to incorporate into its plot the themes of political rebellion and street revolutions. As with this example, in many instances we feel that events occur in the novel, like natural phenomena, without any reference to human agency. Human beings, it appears, do not choose their lives: they suffer or enjoy life according to a script that they have not written and which they must nonetheless faithfully interpret. The love between Marius and Cosette, for example, is born thus: "Fate, with its mysterious and fatal patience, was slowly bringing together the two languid beings, charged with the tempestuous electricity of passion . . ." (IV, III, VI, p. 914).

This *prodigious skill of chance*, as the narrator calls it when referring to the Battle of Waterloo (II, I, XVI, p. 362), does not simply restrain or affect the lives of individuals; societies as well have their destinies mapped out. The great events of history obey a complicated, ineluctable destiny. The defeat that Napoleon suffers at Waterloo is, according to the divine stenographer, due to a series of accidents: "The rainy night, the Hougomont wall, the sunken lane at Ohain, Grouchy deafened by cannon fire, the guide who misled Napoleon, and the guide who helped Bülow—the whole cataclysm is marvelously directed" (II, I, XVI, p. 362). And in those same admirable pages that re-create— that invent—the tragedy of Waterloo, we are told that the Revolution will survive the defeat since it was a "providential and wholly inevitable event" (II, I, XVII, pp. 363–364).

History is predetermined by a divine will that is manifested through "chance," through sudden, spasmodic incidents, unintelligible to those who suffer their consequences, and which together lead progressive humanity rather confusedly toward moral redemption, toward reconciliation with God.

These providential incidents are unforeseen and continually disorder and reorder people's lives without much reference to their own free will. They are either positive or negative, depending on whether they bring fortune or misfortune, but from a novelistic point of view they all have equal weight because they all keep the plot wheels turning, and keep the reader involved and engaged. For example, it is by chance that when he is fleeing from the implacable Javert with Cosette on his back through the shadowy streets of Paris, and he climbs the wall of a mysterious building in the Petit Picpus neighborhood, Jean Valjean should meet old Fauchelevent working as a gardener in what turns out to be a convent. Jean Valjean had saved the old man's life, and, out of eternal gratitude, Fauchelevent will help him to hide away in this limbo for the following five years. However, can one conceive of a more unhappy coincidence than when Fauchelevent supposedly takes the body of Mother Crucifixion—he is in fact smuggling out Jean Valjean—to be buried at the Vaugirard cemetery, and finds that his friend Mestienne, the gravedigger, has just died and has been replaced by an unknown workman? The chapter ends with a question that leaves the reader open-mouthed: will Jean Valjean be buried alive? (II, VIII, V, p. 568). It is a very useful coincidence that when the former galley slave goes to Montfermeil to rescue Cosette, as he promised Fantine, he should find the girl alone and frightened in the wood in the middle of the night, fetching water for Madame Thénardier, because Jean Valjean can discover in this way the cruelty with which the couple treat the orphan girl (II, III, VI, p. 411). And it is an even more extraordinary coincidence that Marius should come across, in a chapel in Saint Suplice, a strange character, Monsieur Mabeuf, the only person in the world who can tell him that his father, Colonel Pontmercy, often came to see him on Sundays in that same chapel, but that he was forced to remain hidden because Marius's grandfather, Monsieur Gillenormand, had forbidden him to make contact with his grandson (III, III, V, pp. 633–644). This revelation is a decisive turning point in Marius's psychological and political development.

does he offer? Why, forty francs, of course (I, V, X, p. 193). However many coincidences occur in the world of the reader, he or she knows quite clearly that chance does not operate in real reality so often and with such precision.

*Coincidence* is one of the fundamental ways of organizing life in fictive reality, and it is through coincidence that the hand of fate can most often be seen at work. This *law of chance* appears in innumerable, isolated examples, but it appears even more clearly as the key element, the very nucleus of three "active craters," or significant scenes, in the novel: what we will call the "irresistible traps."

## The Irresistible Traps

A novel, like a human life, is made up of important events and routine and trivial actions. Unlike what usually happens in a poem or a short story—genres that, owing to their brevity and tight structure, can at times achieve an extraordinary unity, where all the parts have the same conceptual and rhetorical richness—in the novel, a genre that is imperfect on account of its length, its numerous cast, and the influence of time, the episodes that are woven into its structure are inevitably unequal. Some are essential, others are less significant, and others are solely instrumental, mere bridges to link the important events and to ensure the fluidity of narrative time, the illusion that time is passing. In the most significant episodes of a novel—in its *volcanic craters*—life reaches a maximum intensity, and the energy generated reverberates throughout the whole text. We do not need critics to tell us what are the important "craters" in the novels that we love. It is enough for us to close our eyes. Memory brings them back to us intact, intense, and

nostalgic, images that aroused, excited, angered, or sad-
dened us: Captain Ahab disappearing with his obsession,
his mythical prey, the white whale, into the immense ocean;
Don Quixote and Rocinante charging at windmills; the
timid Julien Sorel daring to take Madame Renal's hand
when the clock strikes ten during that evening in the country; the agony and death of Madame Bovary; the castration
of the mulatto Joe Christmas; the ascension of Remedios
the Beauty into heaven; Orlando's sex change; the Professor, the anarchist, wandering the streets of London
strapped with explosives, ready to blow up the police who
are looking to capture him, and himself with them, and so
many others . . . It is not by chance that these images, now
part of our lives, seem, because of their dynamism, complexity, and delicacy, to sum up the novels that they are
taken from, seem to symbolize and synthesize these works.
The vitality that flows from them expands in time and
space, and their emotional charge and power of suggestion
are contagious. These active craters also usually reflect the
novel as a whole in terms of technique and style. By reading them attentively and examining how they work, we can
analyze the narrative structure in greater depth, identifying
the constant features and the variables that organize the
novel. These episodes show most clearly and most effectively how the author constructs his narrative.

The craters that dominate the vast landscape of *Les Misérables*, and affect the whole terrain, are of many different
kinds, but there are three that are similar in nature, and
that occur at key moments in the story, in which the
chance meeting, the surprising coincidence, is accentuated
to such a degree that the novel seems to move onto a fantastic plane. I am referring to the "irresistible traps," those
places—the Gorbeau tenement, the barricade at La Chan-

vrerie, the sewers of Paris—to which the "dark vein of destiny" irresistibly draws the main characters, who, until then, had been isolated from each other. These are very intense locations, stalked by destruction and death, and the meetings that take place there spell imminent catastrophe for the heroes: their murder, their ruin, or their imprisonment. These traps are magnets of fate. By multiplying coincidences to a vertiginous degree, they bring face-to-face people who hate or fear each other, and whose lives, after that meeting, will be profoundly changed. In these irresistible traps, which obey the summons of the law of chance, the separate events of the story are tied together, the action is no longer dispersed, and an order is formed; chaos acquires logic. The surprise, the violence, the heroism, and the ignominy that are conveyed in these vibrant pages make these episodes the high points of the novel.

## The Ambush in the Gorbeau Tenement

In his diatribe against the novel, Barbey D'Aurevilly refers to the fantastic circumstance of having so many people in the Gorbeau tenement and states that this seems to him like "le trou de formicaleo, où doivent tomber tous . . . comme les insectes dans le trou de formicaleo."[1]

The Gorbeau tenement, this rabbit warren of poor people in an isolated and mixed neighborhood of Paris, is one of the recurring stage settings in the novel, where Jean Valjean and Cosette, the Thénardiers, and Marius are marooned at different times in their lives, without knowing of each other's existence. These coincidences are premonitions of the great meeting that they will all have—without Cosette, but with the addition of Javert—in the dark tenement, when Thénardier, alias Jondrette, alias Fabantou, decides to set an ambush to steal two hundred thousand francs from, and doubtless to kill, the naive philanthropist who has fallen into his clutches, Monsieur Leblanc, alias Monsieur Urbain Fabre, alias Jean Valjean. An extraordinary chain of seemingly inconsequential events place Jean Valjean in the path of the innkeeper from Montfermeil, and Thénardier, with the help of a band of ruffians who operate by night in Paris, prepares a trap for him that the ex-convict falls into quite unwittingly. Young Marius, who is in love with Cosette, whom he has seen, then lost, in the Jardin de Luxembourg, is, by chance, a neighbor of the Thénardiers, and he discovers the plot. When he goes to the police station to report the intended crime, the inspector who talks to him is Javert, the only representative of authority able to recognize the fugitive galley slave, whom everyone thinks is dead. But during this intense night, which is full of extraordinary coincidences, one even greater coincidence occurs. Stunned and dismayed, Marius learns that the infamous Jondrette, who has planned Cosette's abduction and the probable murder of Monsieur Leblanc, and whom he is about to hand over to the police, is none other than the man who saved his father at Waterloo, the man decreed by Colonel George Pomerancy's will as the recipient of his son's loyal service.

The appearance of all these people, driven by chance to this dark place, binds together the hitherto disparate stories of each individual into a single story. This crossroads in the plot, where all the threads of the different stories become tied, or retied after being untied for many months or years, raises many dramatic questions: Will Thénardier kill Monsieur Leblanc? Will he kidnap Cosette? Will Jean Valjean pay the ransom? Will Marius discover that Jondrette is the man who saved his father? And when he discovers it, will he give the agreed signal and hand him over to Javert? Will Javert recognize Jean Valjean? The fascination and emotional intensity felt by readers of these narrative "craters" make them turn their attention with increased interest from that episode to what comes before and also after it in the narrative. The emotional charge that flows backward and forward in the narrative from these central events is like a series of concentric waves that join forces with the waves emanating from other narrative craters, and give movement to the whole story, thus achieving what is the greatest ambition of any novel: to offer the illusion of life itself.

## The Barricade at La Chanvrerie

If the instrument that fate uses to bring the protagonists together in the Gorbeau tenement is a sinister individual, the "poor, evil" Thénardier, what brings the main characters to that desolate street in the Saint-Denis neighborhood, to confront each other in the epic setting of an insurrection, is another protagonist in the novel, not a flesh-and-blood character but one that, like suffering and like God, is abstract and anonymous: history. The barricade is another trap, a place surrounded by dangers, whose inhabitants await misfortune: either prison or violent death. But, unlike those in the Gorbeau tenement and the "Entrails of the Leviathan," the people who are there have entered this trap of their own volition, knowing the risks they are running, motivated by spite (Marius), a political ideal (Enjolras), a professional reason (the spy Javert), or a personal one (Jean Valjean). Gavroche's motives are mixed: he shows the curiosity and freshness of a child always on the lookout for adventure and an instinctive solidarity with a cause that, he senses, chimes with his own iconoclastic nature and his popular roots.

We also see in this case the law of chance functioning at great speed, multiplying incidents and coincidences so that these characters can meet on the barricades and their fates can become entwined. Beyond what the episode of the "war between four walls" means from the novel's social and historical point of view—I will address this topic later—the providential meeting of the protagonists in the magnetic trap of La Chanvrerie has momentous consequences in their lives and triggers very important events. Jean Valjean saves the life of his greatest enemy, the bloodhound who has turned his days into a living hell. By so doing, he leaves a tiny trace of moral acid in Javert's conscience that will eat away his certainties and plunge him into doubt, anguish, and suicide. And he also saves Marius, through a mythic feat of strength, knowing all along that Marius is in love with Cosette and that he will take her—the only person Jean Valjean has in the world—away from him. In the midst of a hail of bullets that cut short the existence of the most affectionate and sympathetic character in the novel— the urchin Gavroche, the abandoned son of the Thénardiers, the monarch of the gutter and of mischief making— Jean Valjean saves Marius's life and simultaneously assures the future happiness of the young man and Cosette, and his own unhappiness. As well as adding a political dimension to our fictive society, something that until this moment had put in only a brief appearance—the theme of poverty and misfortune had been developed in moral, religious, and social terms, but not in political terms—the barricade offers a more rounded picture of Javert, revealing him to be more subtle than had previously been thought, and also shows Jean Valjean to be more questioning, making him a much less schematic character than his hagiographer, the narrator, would have us believe.

This is without doubt the largest "crater" in *Les Misérables*, and these are the most compelling pages in the book, in particular, those that cover the fall of the barricade. The attack of the troops, the resistance of the rebels, the acts of individual heroism or skill—Jean Valjean shooting down the mattress to strengthen the barricade under fire from the attackers, Gavroche picking up bullet cartridges impervious to the firing, the assault and capture of the redoubt in an explosion of violence and savagery—are the best-written pages in the novel. The language is extremely powerful, dramatic, and vivid. It is also one of the rare occasions that the narrator forgets himself and the reader forgets him: as if caught up in the magic of the events, the "divine stenographer" disappears behind his characters and the action, and the story becomes self-sufficient. It is the most modern moment in a classical novel.

## The Paris Sewers

The third active crater that is also an irresistible trap—a place of risk endowed with an unsettling and mysterious power of attraction that the protagonists submit to meekly and blindly—is the sewers of Paris and the surrounding area, on the banks of the Seine. The same characters brought together by fate in the Gorbeau tenement—Thénardier, Jean Valjean, Marius, and Javert—meet again, through the workings of chance, in a crucial episode that hastens the ending of the story: the death of Javert, the marriage of Marius and Cosette, and the tragic-glorious death of the galley slave.

Unlike the other episodes, the fortuitous meeting in this section does not occur all at once, but is spaced over three successive moments in which the law of chance brings the characters together and has them ricochet off each other like billiard balls. Javert comes across Thénardier by chance in the docks by the Seine and follows him (V, III, III, pp. 1309–1313). Thénardier goes down into the sewers and meets Jean Valjean at the end of his Dantesque journey through the entrails of the city, carrying Marius, whom he has saved at the fall of the barricade (V, III, VIII, pp. 1325–1330). Thénardier opens the gate out of the sewer to let the ex-convict and the wounded man reach the surface, and they stumble into the light only to fall into the hands of the implacable Javert (V, III, IX. pp. 1330–1332).

Providence in this case, as well as being what the narrator calls "horrible" (V, III, VIII, p. 1326), is also paradoxical. It is the sinister Thénardier who plays the part of the guardian angel by getting Jean Valjean out of the labyrinth, but his freedom is all too brief as he is soon captured by Javert. As well as the dramatic nature of these meetings and the way that they advance the plot, we should add a further element that makes this scene memorable to the reader: its mystery. In the introductory essay to his edition of *Les Misérables*, Marius-François Guyard shows that beneath the disordered appearance of the novel there is a rigorous structure at work: the story develops alternately in the world of action and in the world of the minds or the souls of the characters. The periods of immobility, the long and often distressing parentheses that interrupt the physical action, are, in fact, episodes that explore another type of event that the narrator is as interested in recounting as the objective events themselves: the moral, religious, and political conflicts that take place within the characters. These two planes—the life of the body and the life of the soul—are almost always separated into different chapters, but, on occasion, they come together, to great dramatic effect.

One of the privileged moments in which we witness, simultaneously, certain dramatic events in the exterior, physical life of the characters, and in the secret, intangible, life of their souls, is this threefold meeting in the dark sewers and on the banks of the Seine bathed in the uncertain light of dusk. Neither Thénardier nor Javert recognizes Jean Valjean, covered in the mud and filth of the sewers. The dialogue between the galley slave and the villain is, in truth, a monologue by Thénardier, interspersed with the monosyllabic answers and silences of his interlocutor. Through the questions, statements, and proposals made by Thénardier, we see in a flash of infernal light, which illuminates the malodorous semidarkness, all the vileness of this hyena who, years before, had been in the fields of Waterloo robbing corpses. His homicidal mentality takes for granted that the body which the galley slave is dragging along is someone whom he has robbed and killed, and that he now wants to dispose of the evidence. He immediately fixes a price—half the proceeds—to open the gate to the outside world. But not even with this criminal offer is Thénardier playing honestly, because, apart from keeping the money of the person he presumes is a corpse, he is also giving the presumptive murderer up to Javert, in order to get the policeman off his tail. The stench and the filth of the place reflect Thénardier's nature revealed in all its nakedness, and, by contrast, the nobility of Jean Valjean shines forth all the more brightly.

Does the disgraceful spectacle of Thénardier influence Jean Valjean's decision to reveal his identity to the policeman? His gesture seems that of a demoralized man, weary of running away from, and fighting against, adverse fate, finally resigned to the immense evil of the world. However, despite our sorrow at the former galley slave's despondency, the most disturbing aspect of this meeting between Jean Valjean and Javert takes place within Javert himself. What happens to him? Something strange. Why does he not use the *tu* form as a gesture of contempt toward Jean Valjean, as he has always done previously? Why does he agree to take Marius to his grandfather's house, which, by any definition, is a dereliction of duty, something previously unimaginable for him? Why his sullen silence? In this episode, which once again ties the loose threads of *Les Misérables*, the tale melds the subjective and the objective, the exterior events and the moral drama, offering a unified view of humanity that in other parts of the story seems not to exist.

"I am not like other men; I am in the grip of fate" ("je fais la part de la fatalité"), Victor Hugo wrote to Juliette Drouet.[2] It is difficult to accept this assertion when one knows something of the biography of the author of *Les Misérables*. If something stands out in this multifaceted life of a man who was a poet, a novelist, a journalist, a politician, an academic, a family man, a serial lover, a designer, a spiritualist, a teacher, and a conscience of his society, a man who revolutionized the ethics and customs of his time, it is that "fate" seems to have played a very small part in an existence shaped by determination, dedication, sacrifice, discipline, self-confidence, ambition, fantasy, and, of course, an extraordinary flair for the French language. Victor Hugo is one of those men who, it seems, bring fate to heel: his character and determination appear so strong that he can overcome and use in his favor all the obstacles that chance might place in his way, turning adversity to his advantage. One example among many: instead of depressing him and causing his political demise, his long exile in Belgium, Jersey, and Guernsey enabled him to write his most ambitious books and increased his prestige in society to mythological proportions. The philosophies of freedom, which argue that men and women have absolute control over their destinies, would seem to be able to count Victor Hugo as a striking example of their creed.

In the world of *Les Misérables*, by contrast, fate is always lying in wait, and human beings, unlike the real Victor Hugo, can rarely escape its traps or turn its onslaught into advantage. These providential coincidences, accidents, meetings, and near misses give a fateful direction to their lives. They seem to have little strength to "choose" their destinies in a reality in which we find, as the divine stenographer puts it so well, "that nothing is more imminent than the impossible, and what one must always foresee is the unforeseen" (IV, XIV, V, p. 1163). In a note for the prologue of the novel, written at the end of 1861 and subsequently discarded, Victor Hugo wrote, "This book is nothing more than a protest against the inexorable."[3] Is that what the novel is? The problem stems from the fact that there is no proof—there can be no proof—that in real reality there operates a preestablished design that shapes the lives of men and women like wax figures in a mold, that man is merely a product of superior and uncontrollable forces that dispense in an arbitrary manner fortune and misfortune, greatness and smallness, without the intervention of free will. In the fictive world of *Les Misérables*, by contrast, in instances like the three "craters" we have explored, and on many other occasions, we can see the mark of this "dark vein" of destiny branded on the foreheads of the characters, a fate that will make and break them at will.

reality. Men and women are free at times, in certain circumstances, for fixed periods, for certain things. In other
moments, situations, or matters, they are puppets that are
moved by the hand of fate. There is no rational way of
knowing where the boundaries between these two states
might lie. The same is true for the wider society. Characters cannot define the boundaries between these two
worlds in which they are free or slaves, responsible or irre-
sponsible. Readers are similarly perplexed. Does fate intervene to get Jean Valjean to arrive on time for the trial of
poor Champmathieu, or is it Jean Valjean himself who, by
taking his fate in his own hands, overcomes all the obstacles in his way? One might say that the divine stenographer
is as confused as we are. There are moments, however,
when the presence of this supreme "hand" seems evident
to the character and to the narrator, as on the night when
Jean Valjean and Cosette are fleeing from the Gorbeau
tenement through the streets of Paris with Javert and his
men in pursuit: "Jean Valjean knew no more than Cosette
where he was going. He trusted in God as she trusted in
him. It seemed to him that he, too, had someone greater
than himself holding his hand; he thought he felt an invisible being guiding him" (II, V, I, pp. 463–464). In this case
at least it is clear that it is the "hand" that is guiding the
ex-convict toward the Picpus convent that will offer shelter
to him and to Cosette for the next five years.

And how do events unfold in history and society? In
a programmed way, dictated by the workings of fate, or
through the achievements or failures of sovereign human
beings? Here, once more, the capricious "hand" can be
seen at work, organizing events, or else allowing things to
happen as a result of the wisdom or stupidity, the strength
or the weakness, the kindness or the wickedness of human

beings themselves. Who decides the result of the Battle of Waterloo? Napoleon, Wellington, or a fate whose threads are spun by God in an inscrutable fashion? The divine stenographer appears to prefer the latter option: "If it had not rained in the night of 17–18 June 1815, the future of Europe would have changed. A few more or a few less drops of water were what decided Napoleon's actions. For Waterloo to mark the end of Austerlitz, providence just needed a bit of rain, and an unseasonably cloudy sky was sufficient to cause the collapse of a world" (II, I, III, p. 323). A few pages later, repeating that it was the arrival of Blücher instead of Grouchy on the field of battle that had decided the final result, the narrator exclaims, "These are the immense moments of chance, linked to an infinity that escapes us" (II, I, XI, p. 350). Now, if in this instance it is providence that is determining the course of European history through its infinite vision and omnipotence, what can one say of the other major historical event in the novel, the street uprising of June 1932? In this case, the "hand" appears not to intervene at all and to allow objective events— superior force of arms and superior numbers—to determine the eventual crushing of the insurrection. While Napoleon figures in the novel as a mere puppet of adversity, Enjolras appears to us as someone responsible for what is happening, who lucidly chooses a defeat that he is sure will turn into a posthumous victory.[4]

We can understand why, when faced with such a reality, in which freedom—the power of decision that men and women have over the events that affect their lives—is so random, evasive, fleeting, arbitrary, and volatile, that the characters, like Jean Valjean in prison, might feel insignificant, a grain of sand blown by the wind: "All of this, laws, prejudices, facts, men, and things, came and went above his head in the complex and mysterious movement that God stamps on civilization, walking over him and crushing him with a sort of placid cruelty and inexorable indifference" (I, II, VII, p. 99).

We can also understand that in such a reality, the identities of the characters are as exterior and impermanent as the clothes they wear. To explore this, let us look more closely at the inhabitants of the fiction, who can be described perfectly by the epithet that the narrator uses for Thénardier. Let us look more closely at the "touchy monsters" of the novel (III, VIII, XX, p. 811).

CHAPTER III

# *Touchy Monsters*

When our grandparents wept as they read *Les Misérables*, they thought that the characters moved them to tears because of their touching humanity. But what really moved them was their ideal nature, their manifest inhumanity. The characters appear to be physically normal, but their virtues and vices, and the way they behave, feel, and think, mark them out as different. Apart from Marius, who seems the odd one out in this group, none of the main characters are average, common, easily recognizable men and women. Instead they represent extreme and unusual forms of human behavior: the saint, the righteous man, the hero, the villain, the fanatic. The novel is full of archetypal figures. What in real reality is the norm, in the world of fiction is the exception; instead of average human behavior, we are given caricatures or stereotypes. This shift is clearly evident today to the readers of *Les Misérables*, who can recognize immediately the distance that separates them from the novel's protagonists. Contemporary readers of the novel, by contrast, were not aware of this distance, and both friends and detractors of Victor Hugo agreed that the novel faithfully portrayed them. In a subjective sense, they were right. Fiction described what the men and women of the time wanted or believed themselves to be, characters filtered through the lens of romanticism, which depicted them in a schematic way, as emblems of mutually incompatible virtues or vices. From this standpoint, individual characters embodied one of these schematic principles, without any nuance in their actions. Every age has its own unreality: its myths, its phantoms, its illusions, its dreams, and its ideal vision of human beings that fiction expresses more faithfully than any other genre. To medieval readers, the exploits of Amadis or Esplandián could seem realist because the fabulous adventures expressed their deepest desires. For readers in the romantic era, who expected excess and fervently desired the world to be made up of angels and devils, *Les Misérables* offered them a cast of characters for whom immoderate behavior is the norm and ordinary behavior is the exception.

The divine stenographer assures us that human beings are divided between "the luminous" and "the shadowy," a suggestive image for the good and the evil characters in the novel. But we could also add another division: between superior beings and simple mortals or normal people.

## A Character without Qualities

In *Les Misérables*, the main characters are not people of flesh and blood but rather heroes in the Homeric sense, demigods who transcend human limitations, and whose physical or moral exploits and unswerving behavior—for good or evil—make them seem godlike or demonic. This is true of the good characters, like the bishop of Digne,

Jean Valjean, Gavroche, Monsieur Mabeuf, or Éponine, and of the bad characters, like Javert or the Thénardiers. By contrast, the most human characters in the novel, who show indecision, incoherence, and nuanced or complex actions, seem mediocre in comparison to the more mythical characters. Marius is a good example. In his nondescript, routine existence, he commits one act of bravery—loyal to the memory of his father, he leaves his comfortable life with his grandfather for a more precarious existence—and he shows signs of courage on the La Chanvrerie barricade. But apart from these two instances, he is passive, indecisive, and defeatist, and without Jean Valjean's help, he would have sunk into frustration.

The narrator says of him: "There is a way of falling into error while going in search of the truth. He had a sort of violent sincerity that made him see everything as a whole, without distinction" (III, III, VI, p. 649). Is this an accurate description of Monsieur Gillenormand's grandson? Up to a point. Since Victor Hugo used many details of his own life in Marius's biography, the novel treats the young man with more sympathy than he inspires in the reader. Marius is naive rather than intelligent, egotistical rather than generous, more passive than active, and, at crucial moments, like the ambush at the Gorbeau tenement when he is paralyzed by indecision, or in his egotistical dealings with Jean Valjean, he is simply not up to the task. In a world in which men are valued for their grand gestures, for the theatrical consequences of their actions, the two dramatic initiatives taken by the young man—to break with his uncle and to join the barricade at La Chanvrerie with his friends from the ABC—cannot just be seen as pure, unambiguous, acts. Does he leave the house on a point of principle or out of juvenile stubbornness, the whim of a spoiled child? If he had managed to get hold of the money to go to London and meet Cosette, he probably would not have gone to the barricade. On the barricade, he seems resigned rather than convinced of the cause, a victim of "visionary stupor that always precedes the fateful hour voluntarily accepted" (V, I, IV, p. 1210). It is obvious that he is there not out of political conviction, but because of fatalism and despair. Nor is his ideological conversion very convincing; it seems to be based on the quarrel with his old grandfather, a way of rebelling against family authority, rather than the result of an intellectual process or a moral conviction. For that reason, his political ideals do not prevent him, after a time, from returning to Monsieur Gillenormand's house, making up with him, and, without any pangs of conscience, taking up the life that the old man had marked out for him since his birth. His Jacobin behavior was no more than an adolescent crisis.

And yet, this mediocre and nondescript figure, with all his hesitations and confusion, is the most "realist" character in the novel in that his actions are ambiguous and not obviously predictable, for it is in this ambiguity that we can recognize the unpredictability and relativity of real life. Marius seems of lesser stature because he is merely a man in a world of giants, because his actions are not grandiose, unlike the grandiose goodness of Jean Valjean, the bishop of Digne, or Gavroche, the grandiose evil of Thénardier, or the grandiose fanaticism of Javert. Instead his actions are ambivalent and lacking in that most essential characteristic of the romantic world: theatricality. Like all flesh-and-blood beings, Marius is a contradictory person, both generous and egotistical, someone who cannot foresee whether his actions will have a positive or negative impact. When it comes to Cosette and the memory of his dead father, Marius is capable of energy, sacrifice, and heroism. But he behaves in a cold and even cruel way toward his grandfather and Jean Valjean. This ambiguity should make us sympathetic toward him, since he is so much like us, but instead, we find him irritating and unreal. Compared with the convincing heroes that surround him and demand our love and attention through their eloquence, Marius's normality seems abnormal. His example shows us once again that fiction is not life but is in conflict with life: it is a life apart with its own laws and rules, in which, as in the case of Marius, excess seems normal to us and "realism" seems completely unreal.

Speaking of the evil characters in the story, the divine stenographer calls them monsters ("In case you had not realized, even the vilest creatures have their susceptibilities, even monsters are touchy," III, VIII, XX, p. 811). But monstrosity—inhumanity—is not an attribute of the evil characters alone, for it applies equally to the good. Almost all the characters seem to possess an instinct that is stronger than their intelligence or their reason, and that leads them to good or evil: "It would seem that certain men possess a real bestial instinct, pure and integral like all instincts, that creates antipathies and sympathies, that fatally separates one nature from another, that does not hesitate or become disturbed, that does not remain silent or become confused, that is always clear in its obscurity, infallible, imperious, resistant to any intelligent advice or reason, and that, whatever way the die is cast, will secretly alert the dog-man to the presence of the cat-man and the fox-man to the presence of the lion-man" (I, V, V, pp. 176–177). Indeed, throughout the story we see the way that these relationships of love and hate, friendship and antipathy, occur instantaneously. Marius and Cosette fall in love without speaking a word to each other. Javert has a feeling that

Monsieur Madeleine is a potential prey long before any evidence emerges to justify his suspicions. Jean Valjean senses intuitively the love between Marius and Cosette. Marius becomes part of the ABC group of friends by a sort of osmosis. Within minutes of meeting the mysterious visitor who has come to take Cosette away, Thénardier senses that he "was dealing with someone very strong" (II, III, IX, p. 436). On issues of morality, above all, the characters give the impression that they take the right or the wrong road by instinct. André Maurois observed that Victor Hugo was "obsessed by Manichaean dualism," that he could see things only in black and white, which is why he made his characters either sublime or grotesque, hence their monstrosity.[1] He is right; a Manichaean vision permeates the novel: in the fictive reality there are good and bad people and almost no one in between (Marius is one of these exceptions). It is true that, as happens with Jean Valjean, a man can be evil and then become righteous, but this change does not alter the ethical dichotomy that divides the human species. What we do not find in this fictive universe are characters that, as happens in the real world, are ambiguous, morally contradictory, and capable of both good and evil. This Manichaean vision, which frequently occurs in romantic literature, has its roots in the exemplary tales of medieval literature, in which God and the Devil were always in opposition through third parties, and God always emerged victorious. But within this overall generalization, other factors establish subtle differences in the broad classification that divides good from evil in *Les Misérables*.

### The Saint

Monseigneur Bienvenu Myriel and Jean Valjean, who are on the side of the righteous, could not be more different. It requires an enormous, and frequently tragic, struggle for the ex-convict to achieve goodness, while goodness flows from Monseigneur Bienvenu—and from Éponine and Gavroche—as naturally as perspiration. He is without a doubt the least touchy of all the monsters.

Monseigneur Bienvenu embodies one idea: sanctity. He was a prosperous man of the world in his youth, he married young and spent time in Italy in exile, and we do not know whether, as a layman, he was a sinner who experienced a conversion. From the moment we see him in the novel, as a priest in Digne, having been appointed a bishop there as a result of a memorable remark that he made to the emperor in a chance meeting in Paris, his personality is all of a piece. He is absolutely dedicated to a life of compassion, sympathy, and generosity to others. The tiny stain that marks his pristine spirit is his pleasure at eating with the silver cutlery that remained from his former possessions, a pleasure which, we hear him say, "I would find difficult to give up" (I, I, VI, p. 38). In fact he gives them up very easily when it is a question of releasing Jean Valjean, who has stolen the cutlery, from police custody. In order to make him human, with a few traces of imperfection, the divine stenographer reproaches him for having been "glacial" with the emperor in his period of decline. But even his inoffensive anti-Bonapartism is moderated by generous deeds, as when he employs as a caretaker in the cathedral a penniless soldier, who had lost his previous job for making fun of Louis XVIII (I, I, XI, p. 53).

Monseigneur Bienvenu is kindhearted, calm, and gentle. He is a good judge when it comes to matters of the spirit, he is an optimist who is convinced of the inexorable triumph of good over evil, and he prefers to preach by example instead of on the pulpit. He is an agreeable old man, quick-witted and humorous. Nothing makes him angry or upsets his equilibrium. When the materialist senator delivers his provocative speech, arguing that "God is fine for the masses," while rich and refined people should be governed instead by principles of pleasure and enjoyment, the prelate smiles at him and congratulates him on his philosophy (I, I, VIII, p. 34). And when he discovers that a former member of the Revolutionary Convention, whom the whole of Digne hates, is a good man, he does not hesitate in asking for his blessing, as if he were a saint.[2]

Completely nonsectarian and nondogmatic, this Catholic is a tolerant man who is capable of entertaining other points of view. He is not in any way a forerunner of the progressive priests of the twentieth century who would identify religion with social and political action, embrace revolution—sometimes Marxism—and look to marry Christ with Marx in liberation theology. Monseigneur Bienvenu is not a revolutionary, he is a saint, and his personality can be seen to stem from the exemplary stories of the catechism and popular religion. Any form of violence is contrary to his nature as is any political ideology and, indeed, any attempt to offer an intellectual rationalization of faith. For him, faith is a question of feelings and love rather than ideas; it is impulse, emotion, giving, action, rather than theory and doctrine. His benevolent figure would seem to fit into a Catholic tradition of men and women—like Abbé Pierre and Mother Teresa—who selflessly follow the evangelical message of commitment to the meek of the earth, irrespective of ideology.

In her *Journal d'exil*, Adèle Hugo remarks that when the family met in Marine Terrace in Jersey, as Victor Hugo was about to start work again on the novel that he had put aside in 1848 ("because of the revolution"), he had heated discussions with his son Charles about the character of

Monseigneur Bienvenu. Charles Hugo attacked the priests as "enemies of democracy" and regretted that his father was making the bishop of Digne "a prototype of perfection and intelligence." He suggested that instead of having a priest, he should invent someone "with a liberal, modern profession, like a doctor . . ." Victor Hugo's reply was blunt: "I cannot put the future into the past. My novel takes place in 1815. For the rest, this Catholic priest, this pure and lofty figure of true priesthood, offers the most savage satire on the priesthood today . . . I am not interested in the opinion of blind and stupid republicans. I am only concerned to do my duty . . . Man needs religion. Man needs God. I say it out loud, I pray every night . . ."[3] This is another of the bishop of Digne's functions in the novel: he exemplifies the Christianity that Hugo believed in, and the spirituality of the church ministers. In his vast introductory essay to the novel, which he eventually did not include in the published version, "Philosophie, commencement d'un livre," Victor Hugo exhorted the reader to read *Les Misérables* as a "religious book."

The main function of the bishop of Digne in the novel is to act as a catalyst for the ex-convict Jean Valjean to change from an evil man into a good man. This conversion, which is similar but not identical to Javert's conversion, which is sparked off by Jean Valjean's goodness and nobility, is the most important event in the story, since the most decisive events in the novel all stem from it. For that reason, even though Monseigneur Bienvenu disappears physically in the first part of the novel, he remains an invisible presence, like a halo, that accompanies the ex-convict through the vicissitudes of his life. This presence shines forth symbolically in the final episode, in the light from the candlesticks that Jean Valjean has beside his deathbed.

These candlesticks are proof that he has remained faithful, to the very end, to the pledge he made to Bishop Myriel to act as a righteous man.

## The Just Man

Jean Valjean is the central character in *Les Misérables*, a character as excessive as the narrator himself. Marius correctly observes, "He is absolutely courageous, virtuous, heroic, and saintly" (V, IX, V, p. 1478). The ex-convict's physical strength is prodigious. He can lift the cart that is squashing old Fauchelevent on his back like Atlas, pick Marius up one-handed when the young man has fainted on the barricade, and carry him for hours through the entrails of the Leviathan. These are the actions of a colossus. The last exploit is all the more surprising when we realize that—he had been born in 1768, and the funeral of General Lamarque that sparked the uprising took place in June 1832—he was then sixty-five years old. Then there is his admirable agility, when he rescues the sailor from Toulon hanging from the top of a mast or when he climbs the vertical wall of the convent of Petit Picpus with little Cosette on his back, to escape the clutches of Javert. These feats of Jean Valjean bring to mind other fictional heroes, especially Vautrin in Balzac's *Les Illusions perdues*. Apart from the similarity in names, Valjean and Vautrin are alike in other ways: their physical strength, their imprisonment, their mysterious appearances and disappearances, the changing names (Abbot Herrera in *La Comédie humaine* is Monsieur Madeleine in *Les Misérables*), and their lack of carnal desires.

But unlike Vautrin, who is unscrupulous, Jean Valjean is

intrinsically moral. Condemned to the galleys for having stolen a loaf of bread, Valjean repeatedly attempts escape, causing his sentence to be extended to nineteen years. In prison he is known for his unsociable nature, his strength, and his solitary behavior rather than for his cruelty. It is only when he is freed and arrives in Digne, is mistreated by innkeepers and offered lodging by the generous bishop, that we see proof of his bad side: he steals the silver cutlery from the bishop and the forty-sou coin from the boy Petit Gervais outside Digne. The bishop's magnificent act of generosity changes him. From that moment on, Jean Valjean begins a life of abnegation, self-sacrifice, and generosity that, at the end of his days, will make him a Savior of sorts: "The convict became transformed into Christ" (V, IX, IV, p. 1475).

Does the character of Jean Valjean evolve? We have no sense of any process taking place, that he is following a path full of twists and turns—doubts, amendments, mistakes, changes—that will lead him away from error and toward the truth. Instead, we witness a conversion, a sudden, fateful change. The crises that he suffers are not because he finds it difficult, during the "Champmathieu affair" or in his relationship with Marius, to recognize his moral obligations and the correct course of action to be taken. He feels anguish when he imagines the consequences of these actions: his return to prison or his losing Cosette. Jean Valjean suffers but he never wavers. His agony never leads him to question his ethical commitment, which is as clear to him as the law is to Javert. The fact that the morality he tries to live by demands of him sacrifices as inhuman as returning to the prison where he has already spent half his life for an insignificant crime, or losing the child who is the only person he has in the world, does not cause Jean

Valjean to reassess his ethical standpoint. It leads him instead to consider himself weak and imperfect, unable to match up to his own convictions. Is he a stoic? Yes, of course. Perhaps a masochist as well. In addition, Jean Valjean has a good brain: he invents an industrial process that makes him rich, and he surprises the inhabitants of Montreuil-sur-mer with his knowledge of agriculture (like what use can be made of stinging nettles).

While for Monseigneur Bienvenu and Gavroche, goodness is a source of happiness and vitality, for Jean Valjean, to be good and righteous is an anguished choice, which puts his life at risk, subjects him to psychological conflict and torture, and turns him into a rather gloomy, humorless person. He has a tender love for Cosette and he shows a limitless generosity toward his fellow men, but it would be hard to say that he loves life. What we often see in his behavior is a kind of Freudian death wish. He inflicts suffering on himself with the argument—the excuse?—that he needs to atone for his sins. It is true that he had a deprived childhood, that he was given an overwhelmingly harsh prison sentence, and that prison deprived him of joy and vitality. Yet, even taking into account all the reasons that turned Jean Valjean into a lone wolf, there is still a gap between him and ordinary mortals, a distance that separates human beings from monsters, be they angels or devils. His story is moving and his tolerance toward his executioners fills us with admiration. But he seems so distant from us ordinary mortals that we do not feel for him the fondness and sympathy that we have for a character like Gavroche. Jean Valjean's excessive humanity makes him somewhat inhuman.

An air of mystery that we can never quite penetrate surrounds the ex-convict. There are extremes of goodness and evil that we cannot comprehend, that have no place in our lives, which make these extreme characters seem unreal to us. Jean Valjean tests this credibility several times in the story, especially in his dealings with Javert. He treats Javert's implacable pursuit with such magnanimity and lack of bitterness that it seems, at times, that he is looking to inflict punishment on himself.

The most mysterious scene in *Les Misérables,* one of its "active craters," takes place during the ambush that the Thénardiers and the band of ruffians from Patron-Minette set for Jean Valjean at the Gorbeau tenement. The ex-prisoner, who is about to be tortured, anticipates his torturers and burns his own arm with a red-hot iron. The reason for this strange action, he tells them, is to show them that he does not fear pain, that there is no physical torment that can force him to do what he does not want to do. Not only the bandits (and Marius, who is spying on the scene from his room) but also we the readers are disconcerted by this gruesome act. What prompts this brutal, boastful display? Is he playing for time? Is it pride? Is it a desperate, hysterical action? It is perhaps a bit of all these things, but it is also a clear demonstration of disciplined self-punishment and sacrifice, of the ascesis that has been the hallmark of Jean Valjean's life ever since the bishop of Digne won him over to the cause of goodness. This behavior, one might say, reflects an innate desire for pain.

This, for him, is the only way to reach God. He says as much to Marius when he confesses to him that he is an ex-convict: "If you want to be happy, sir, you must have no sense of duty, because a sense of duty is implacable. You might say that it punishes you if you have it, but that isn't so. It rewards you because it puts you in hell, where you feel God at your side. We might be ripped apart, but we are at peace with ourselves" (V, VII, I, pp. 1420). His conviction that he can come close to God only by renouncing all forms of happiness leads him, once Javert has disappeared and he is now out of danger, to leave Cosette, the person he loves most in this world, and sink into a lonely existence. In Jean Valjean, goodness and sanctity are seen in somewhat unnatural terms.

More than a man, Jean Valjean is a superman who stands out through his strength and talent and also through his capacity to embody suffering. So much so that one wonders whether he might not take a secret pleasure in all these misfortunes that befall him, which he feels he must embrace with open arms. Although he is a lay saint—he believes in God and is a religious man, but not a practicing Catholic—his idea of duty coincides with those moralists who are convinced that the road to perfection lies in systematic self-punishment, in emulating the lives of martyrs. This is an old moral standpoint which argues that men and women bring original sin with them into the world, and that they must redeem themselves throughout life, knowing full well that everything, the world and the flesh, will conspire against their redemption, in favor of their fall. Jean Valjean's ascesis and martyrdom might be seen as socially determined, for they are embedded in a historical context in which evil takes the form of laws, institutions, and certain characters, and in which good, in the same way, appears in the form of other representative individuals. But in *Les Misérables*, history and social relations are a facade that, in different guises, represents the ancestral fight to the death between two timeless metaphysical and religious principles: good and evil, God and the Devil, heaven and hell. Jean Valjean is not a rebel; his heroism lies in the humility with which he obeys the law, even though his own life is a striking example of the injustice of the law and of the contradiction between the law of Caesar and the law of God. The ex-convict does not dream of rejecting the principles that structure society, or of the need to change them. Instead he sees the injustice of the world as the result of inevitable human imperfection, and that his response must be one of resignation, abnegation, and sacrifice. He practices these virtues throughout his life with such extreme self-sacrifice and heroism that they seem suspicious. At the end of his life when, obeying a moral imperative, he leaves Cosette, the narrator describes his tragedy in the following terms: "He had, of his own volition, successively given up all his happiness; and having lost Cosette in entirety in one day, he had the misery of losing her once again bit by bit" (V, VIII, III, p. 1444). In his search for perfection, the former galley slave scourges himself, just as much as others scourge him. Such behavior can be explained only by a conviction that man is by nature perverse, and that the only way that he can improve himself is through pain, or else that he derives a tortuous gratification, a morbid pleasure, in this constant humiliation and derision. We should not exclude the possibility that these two reasons are, in fact, one and the same.

## A Puritan World

As well as being touchy, the monsters in *Les Misérables* are usually also chaste. According to Henri Guillemin, all Victor Hugo's main characters are virgins: Jean Valjean, Gilliatt, Gwynplaine, Cimurdain . . . But in none of his other novels is chastity such a feature of his central characters as it is in *Les Misérables*, in which Jean Valjean, Javert, and the leader of the barricade, Enjolras, are seen as sexless beings, not interested in women. Even Marius and Cosette, who share an intense love, seem to be immunized against sex, this demon that only the moral dregs like the Thénardiers succumb to, and which causes the ruin and suffering of poor Fantine.

Chastity is a supreme virtue; it is also the price paid for health and physical strength. The narrator emphasizes this when he describes Jean Valjean: "His strength that, as we know, was prodigious and so little diminished with age, thanks to his chaste and sober life . . ." (V, III, IV, p. 1313). Javert's strength is also notable—his mere presence cows the ruffians in the Gorbeau tenement—and he, like Valjean, has never had a wife, a lover, or the slightest affection for women. The revolutionary Enjolras, who leads the rebellion on the barricades at La Chanvrerie—a pure soul, a fanatical republican, an idealistic Jacobin—has done without sex, as if sex might make him stray from his ideals and deprive him of the physical and moral strength needed for the political struggle. In those fevered hours on the barricade, Bossuet remarks that all the men have mistresses, and that these women make them brave. He adds: "And Enjolras has no woman. He is not in love and he finds the means to be brave. It is unheard-of to be cold as ice and also hot as fire" (V, I, XIV, p. 1237). The narrator hastens to correct Bossuet. Enjolras does not have a woman, but he does have a mistress: the motherland. The abstract lovers for which Jean Valjean and Javert have sacrificed flesh-and-blood women are, for Valjean, the duty that leads him to God and, for Javert, justice and the law.

Love and sex appear as weaknesses that the main protagonists of the story—the monsters—do not succumb to, so that they can be in peak physical and moral condition to carry out their mission, be it the search for God, the ful-fillment of the law, or the revolutionary struggle. The need to mate or carnal desires are attributes of the mediocre characters, mere human beings, who are usually made to pay dearly for the sensuality of love by the "dark vein of destiny." Such is the case of poor Fantine. She had been born in Montreuil-sur-mer, an anonymous working-class girl without any known parents, and at the age of fifteen she had gone to Paris. This pretty girl with beautiful teeth falls in love with the bohemian Tholomyès, gives herself to him, becomes pregnant, and is abandoned by him. And what a penance faces the beautiful Fantine for having given way to the temptation of physical love. She will be exploited mer-cilessly by the Thénardiers, in whose care she has left her daughter; she will be dismissed for being a single mother, condemned to being a beggar and a prostitute, forced to sell her hair and her teeth, and condemned, finally, to die young without ever seeing little Cosette again. What disasters fol-low from a sin of the flesh! On the matter of sex, the moral-ity of *Les Misérables* melds perfectly with the most intolerant and puritanical interpretation of Catholic morality.

This can be seen quite clearly in the love affair between Marius and Cosette, who belong to a world of mediocrity in the fiction—the world of ordinary people—and are thus prone to states like love that the monsters are unaffected by. Now the love between these two is completely ethereal; the sex drive has been surgically removed so that their rela-tionship can be purely one of feeling. Before the wedding the young people exchange one kiss, which is not repeated because, as the narrator says, neither Marius nor Cosette was aware of the existence of carnal desire. When, in one of their meetings, Cosette bends down to pick something up and her corset gapes to reveal her neck, Marius immediately looks away: "There was a gulf that they did not seek to cross, not because they respected it, but because they did not know it existed" (IV, VIII, I, p. 1027). The dialogue between these two virtuous lovers is as unreal as their amorous behavior. For this reason, the episodes where the two lovers talk to each other are the most artificial moments in the novel.

It goes without saying that Marius and Cosette, who had not known love before they met, arrive at the altar as virgins. Their wedding takes place on 16 February 1833, the date when Victor Hugo and his lover Juliette Drouet celebrated their first night of love. When he came to write this episode, Victor Hugo blended in the fiction his first night of love with his lover with the first night with his wife, Adèle Foucher, which had taken place eleven years earlier, on 12–13 October 1822. For on his wedding night, the young twenty-year-old Victor Hugo was a virgin, like Marius. At that time he firmly believed that sex was allowed only within marriage. He wrote as much to Adèle Foucher, during their engagement, on 23 February 1822: "I would think very little of a young woman who would marry a man without having the moral conviction that, because of his principles and character, this man is not only decent but also, and I deliberately use the correct word with all its force, that he is a *virgin*, as virginal as she . . ." (the emphasis is Hugo's).

Does this mean that in his adolescence and as a young man the author of *Les Misérables* was as ethereal and spiritual in matters of love as Marius and the monsters of his novel, and that, in *Les Misérables*, he re-created a world of innocence, with a holy terror of temptations of the flesh, like the world of his early years? If this were the case, then we would have to talk of his nostalgia for a distant past, because it is well known that, along with his youth, the ideal of sexual purity disappeared from Hugo's life and was replaced by an excessive sexual incontinence. If we can believe the testimony of Madame Juana Richard Lesclide,[4] on his wedding night with Adèle Foucher, the young poet began to make up for lost time by making love nine times to his new bride! This improbable feat, apparently, instilled in Madame Victor Hugo a premature aversion to sex. It seems that she resigned herself to having sex without much feeling of joy and for not many years because, after the birth of their fifth child, she did not make love to her husband again on the grounds that she did not want any more children. (Her affair with Sainte-Beuve seems to have been more an act of resentment and a desire for revenge than a genuine passion.)

Victor Hugo, by contrast, continued having sex, with a brio that gives the lie to the philosophy propounded in *Les Misérables* whereby physical and spiritual force exists in inverse proportion to the exercise of the pleasures of the flesh. In his case, sex, physical strength, and creativity were in harmony and were mutually supportive. However, in his study, *Hugo et la sexualité*, Henri Guillemin points out that at the times when he was working most intensively on the novel, the sexual appetite of the great man diminished: "... for example, when he was working furiously on correcting the proofs of the first two volumes of the novel, it was only very infrequently that he noticed a women and stroked her absentmindedly on the cheek, like a man thinking about something else ..."[5]

In any event, the way that *Les Misérables* outlaws and demonizes sex is in stark contrast to the behavior of its author who, once he had given up his adolescent chastity, had an intense sex life with his wife, with Juliette Drouet, with numerous lovers and chance encounters, and who, well into old age, continued having sex with women from all walks of life. His years in exile, in Jersey and Guernsey, where he was accompanied by Juliette Drouet—he could see her house from the tower of Hauteville House, where he did his writing—have been called "the servant years" by his biographers, for reasons that are self-explanatory. He went to bed with servants, or merely fondled them or watched them naked, and he would pay different rates for these services. Thanks to the register of payments that he kept—Victor Hugo was well known for being careful with money—we have a firsthand account of his sexual diversions at the time when—as a moral exorcism or as a *mea culpa?*—he was writing his vindication of asexuality, *Les Misérables*.

The universal law, according to which novelists re-create the world in their novels in the image and likeness of their personal demons, is flexible and subtle and can admit strange twists. In *Les Misérables*, the world of sex has been invented out of a nostalgia for a remote childhood and adolescence in which Victor Hugo was—or wanted to be—a young man as pure as the unreal Marius, and out of a secret, irrational, rejection of the carnal desires that possessed him all his life. What better proof is there that a novel is a form of re-creation and exorcism for the person who writes it and, often, for the person who reads it.

## The Fanatic

After Jean Valjean, the most important monster in *Les Misérables*—and perhaps the most remarkable character that Victor Hugo created—is Javert, the policeman. For most critics, he is the cold, evil character in the novel. The narrator thinks the same, although he always calls him "just," "pure," and "incorruptible." Of course he is not a sympathetic character, but if we analyze him dispassionately, we have to recognize that this man, who was born in prison, the son of a fortune-teller and a poor devil condemned to the galleys, has spent his life obeying the law and making others obey it. He takes this task to fanatical and aberrant extremes. Now, is it Javert's fault that the law is bad? For the policeman, there is a simple equation: thanks to his work, life is organized and society is possible; without him, life would disintegrate into chaos.

Javert's philosophy, which rests on two simple tenets—a respect for authority and a hatred of all forms of rebellion—is admirably summed up in a remark to Monsieur Madeleine: "God knows, it's easy to be good; the hard thing is to be just" (I, VI, II, p. 220). The narrator, who is a romantic, hates the law: he prefers impulses, individual acts, to the collective norm. Javert, like the judge in Camus's *L'Étranger*, puts justice before life, and the narrator puts life before justice. Both, without knowing it, are aware that the two things are incompatible. What is necessary, risky, unjust, inevitable, and also inhuman in the relationship between the law and life itself is best illustrated in the meeting between Javert and Jean Valjean at the bedside of the dying Fantine (I, VIII, III, p. 303). He fulfills his duty, arrests the ex-convict, and tells Fantine the truth about Cosette: this kills the unfortunate woman.

Javert's moment of greatness comes on the barricades, in the middle of the insurrection: here he truly lives up to his monster status. Gavroche recognizes him and Enjolras interrogates him to find out whether he is a *mouchard* (a spy). Javert replies immediately that he is a "representative of the authorities." The narrator states that the policeman "raised his head with the intrepid serenity of a man who has never lied" (IV, XII, VII, p. 1137). Javert's courage compares favorably to that shown by Enjolras. When the insurgents tell him that he will be shot two minutes before the barricade falls, he asks them why they do not execute him straightaway: "We're conserving our ammunition." "Then do it with a knife" (IV, XII, VII, p. 1137). Touchy, let us not forget, means proud, haughty. Despite the fact that they are in opposite camps, Javert's way of thinking, despite his narrowness, is not very different from that of Enjolras, the revolutionary. They have no doubts, they believe blindly in one truth—in one justice—and they are willing to sacrifice life, their own or other people's, for this principle. They are two fanatics, from the right and from the left of the political spectrum.

What does Javert represent? The police? No, something much bigger: human civilization, those rules, laws, taboos, and rites that human beings have to respect in order to live communally. If they violate these rules, there is the danger that society will be plunged into anarchy, become a jungle where only the strong survive. Javert represents human reason as opposed to instinct and imagination, social justice as opposed to individual freedom, the rights of the society as opposed to those of the individual. There is something about him that we find repugnant, even though we recognize that his work is absolutely necessary for the survival of the community. Is it because he is a policeman? No, that is just an appearance. It is because he symbolizes the mutilation—the repression of instinct and irrational desires, the codification and bridling of fantasy and desire—that is the price we must pay for social life to be possible. Romanticism is a movement that, somewhat obscurely, recognizes the *maudit* aspects of human behavior, as Bataille calls them—instinct, unreason, desires, life as excess and waste—and, in the character of Javert, Hugo embodied, with marvelous intuition, that social straitjacket which is both indispensable and intolerable in our paradoxical lives.

Javert is also, like Jean Valjean, a superman, a paragon of virtue taken to unreal extremes. Because of his dogged adherence to norms, he does not hesitate to go against his own interests, as when he asks Monsieur Madeleine to punish him for having doubted him, the mayor, his superior. His courage is at times astonishing. He does not think twice about risking his life by joining the barricade to spy on the revolutionaries, where he is indeed captured and condemned to death. He does not blink an eyelid when the order for his execution comes, and, when he hears that Jean Valjean is claiming the privilege of killing him, he murmurs, "that's fair" (V, I, XVIII, p. 1255). He is a good loser, as ice-cold in defeat as in victory. And his sense of duty is overwhelming. After his brush with death in La Chanvrerie, as soon as Jean Valjean releases him, he rushes to the Préfecture de Police, gives his report, and then "immediately returned to his duties" (V, III, IX, p. 1331). Because, the narrator tells us, when he was on the barricade, tied up, waiting to be executed, Javert "had observed everything, heard everything, understood everything, and retained everything . . ."; "he kept on spying even though he was on the verge of death . . . ," because he was "a first-class spy" (V, III, IX, pp. 1332–1333).

Perhaps the most intense and complex episode of the novel takes place in book 4 of the fifth part: "Javert in Disarray." This upright, one-dimensional man, who seemed to be made of stone, is now full of doubts, and the world that had up to then seemed so logical and simple now becomes impossibly complex. What does Javert discover through Jean Valjean? That the law and morality can be different, even in conflict. That, by letting the galley slave go free, he has acted according to his feelings and against his reason. That he has preferred the confused, unwritten moral law of his individual conscience, which led him to return a favor to the man who had saved his life on the barricade, over written law, social law, which required that the fugitive be returned to prison. Javert, the narrator tells us, has understood that good exists, that God exists. In fact, he has discovered the existence of contradictory truths, of incompatible values, the inexorable confusion between good and evil that occurs in certain human experiences. To realize that good and evil are not, as he had once believed, rigidly separate and recognizable, but rather paths that crisscross, and at times merge into each other, overwhelms Javert and produces the "conversion" that leads him to kill himself. The most terrible thing that happens to him is the discovery that there is something that he cannot control within himself, a feeling that clouds his reason. His death, in the swirls and torrents of the Seine, is similar to that of another of Victor Hugo's monsters, the evil dwarf Habibrah in *Bug-Jargal*, who also, it might be argued, commits suicide in the depths of the Dominican jungle. "He told himself that it was true then, that there were exceptions, that authority could be wrong, that the rules might not be enough, that not everything could be explained by the code of law. That the unpredictable could make itself be obeyed, that the virtue of a convict could set a trap for the virtue of a servant of the state. That monstrosity could be divine, that destiny could set such traps, and, he thought desperately, that he himself had not been immune to surprises" (V, IV, I, p. 1347).

Like Porthos at the end of Alexandre Dumas's saga of the musketeers, Javert dies on the first day in his life that he has doubts, when a breath of humanity shakes his granite personality. His suicide could not be more tragic. Nobody understands him, starting with himself. His superiors think that it was a fit of madness, and even Jean Valjean, the man who made him human and thus plunged him into despair, also thinks that Javert killed himself "because he was mad." The most important action in Javert's life is misunderstood by the entire world.

## An Angel with a Dirty Face

If this very lengthy novel were just full of these spectacular and gloomy titans like Jean Valjean, Javert, or the Thénardiers, then it would be difficult for readers to get through it without feeling overwhelmed. Fortunately they are counterbalanced by other characters who are more vital, joyful, tender, ridiculous, or delightful, like Marius's grandfather, Monsieur Mabeuf, or, most memorable of all, Gavroche, the Paris urchin.

Gavroche is one of Hugo's immortal creations, one of the most appealing and tender characters in fiction. From the time when *Les Misérables* was first published up to now, Gavroche has become indelibly engraved on the readers' memory and has become a mythical creature spanning different languages, countries, and time periods. His relatively brief presence in the story brings a breath of happiness and humanity, a love of life, wit, goodness, and courage in the face of adversity. His purity of spirit is strengthened rather than diminished by poverty, homelessness, and injustice. Biologically he is the son of the revolting Thénardiers, but his real progenitors are the *pícaros* of Spanish Golden Age literature, a Buscón or a Lazarillo, from whom he has inherited his relaxed manner, his cunning, and his survival instincts. He is also a born rebel against laws and institutions, which he instinctively knows are put in place to rob him of his freedom. But although Gavroche shares with the protagonists of the picaresque novel a restless individualism and seditious tendencies, he has not become morally callused in the Darwinian struggle to survive in a society that has marginalized him. Quite the reverse. What is attractive about his personality is that, without setting out to do so, and without realizing what he is doing, he manages to show kindness to everyone he meets, while he is living by his wits. He has to struggle hard to live, but he is not aware of this because he has turned his life into one of those dangerous games that children love to play. Living inside the Elephant of the Bastille kills two birds with one stone. It offers Gavroche shelter against the rain and cold, and, at the same time, it turns his nights into one long risky and spectacular game.

If Javert personifies a man of order, subject to, and obedient to, the checks and balances that make social coexistence possible, then Gavroche is the embodiment of the unruly and marginal individual, who defends his independence and the integrity of his existence against laws and regulations. He shows, in his brief and luminous existence, that official justice, the justice of the authorities and the establishment, masks a profound injustice that causes thousands of human beings to suffer abuse and to be forgotten. Living on the margins of the law, Gavroche does not harm anyone. Instead, he offers assistance to his fellows and helps, albeit minimally, to alleviate the suffering and injustice of *les misérables*. Gavroche is, in his picaresque way, a social crusader.

But more than his goodness, it is the Paris urchin's irrepressible good humor that we find captivating. He always has a merry song on his lips, or a witty, sardonic remark that can defuse the most tense situations and create vitality, enjoyment, and enthusiasm around him, even in the gloomiest of circumstances, as when he is called upon to help the band of ruffians from Patron-Minette to escape. Gavroche's greatest moment of gallantry and humanity comes when he defies death by leaving the shelter of the barricade to gather up cartridges that are essential for the rebel cause. His death is one of the most tragic moments of the novel, and it is also a premonition of the impending massacre in which almost all the rebels led by Enjolras at La Chanvrerie will perish.

Gavroche is sublime proof that in fictional reality good and evil are not hereditary. The son of two diabolical beings, the Thénardiers, the child was born an archangel, the prototype of that long line of "angels with dirty faces," good children from the gutter, forced to live in a malevolent environment, who populate so many twentieth-century novels and films.

Good and evil are essences, part of man's makeup, that, in exceptional circumstances, can change their balance within a person, as happens with Jean Valjean. Nothing of the sort, of course, happens to the Thénardiers. From the moment the tavern owner appears in the story, as a scavenging animal on the fields of Waterloo, stealing from corpses, until he disappears to America, involved in the horrors of the slave trade, all his acts, thoughts, and plans demonstrate his perverse nature, his lack of scruples, and his cruelty, and reveal him to be a human excrescence, a criminal figure of the night. Although a less rounded figure than her husband, Thénardier's wife complements his complete lack of feeling and humanity. The way that Madame Thénardier treats Cosette shows us that there are no limits to this woman's cruelty.

And yet these "terrible parents" have engendered not only the magnificent Gavroche, but also the delicate and kind-hearted Éponine, another one of these fictional beings mysteriously touched by the grace of God. Her secret love for Marius, about which even the talkative narrator does not speak, allowing it instead to be revealed delicately through the girl's behavior, is one of the novel's most subtle motifs. The Thénardiers' two daughters have literary names. Their mother read romantic and sentimental novels and chose the names Éponine and Azelma from these novels. As well as being a good and a tragic character, Éponine also has a ghostly quality to her, as Pierre Albouy has observed.[6] Éponine is described in the novel in a phantasmagorical way; she is more like a ghost than a flesh-and-blood character. Marius spots the two Thénardier girls "in the fog"; he notices them fleeing and disappearing in the darkness and observes that whereas before he had seen them as angelic "jeunes filles," they now seemed like "les goules" (ghouls). Éponine is "akin to the shadows in our dreams"; she comes and goes through the attic "with the boldness of a specter." She is "the messenger from the shadows" who reveals to Marius "a terrifying dimension of the night." She appears suddenly in old Mabeuf's garden, and when he hears her light tread, he thinks he sees a "will-o'-the-wisp." This spectral girl appears to the robbers from Patron-Minette and prevents them from ransacking Cosette's house in the Rue Plumet. This mysterious apparition in the night, with her "spectral bloodshot eyes," "caused the bandits to retreat, believing that they were in the presence of something like the supernatural."

## Collective Characters

The cast of *Les Misérables* is very numerous, almost dizzying if we take into account all the extras who serve as a backdrop to the heroes and the main characters in the different settings—the prison, the convent, the factory, the field of battle, the street revolution—where the novel takes place. To add breadth to this vision and to give the fictive reality an impression of totality, which is the aspiration of all fiction, groups of people, or collective characters, are found alongside the individual characters. These beings function as inseparable parts of a plural identity. They share certain social and psychological traits, like the bohemian students—Blachevelle, Fameuil, Listolier, and Tholomyès—and the high-spirited seamstresses, their lovers—Zéphine, Dahlia, Favourite, and Fantine. They are a gregarious group and it is only at the end of the four couples' outing to the country and their evening's wining and dining that we focus on one of the characters, the future mother of Cosette. Until that moment, and throughout a very long scene, the four young bohemians and the four seamstresses can scarcely be differentiated. They act and speak and enjoy themselves in unison, as if they were all a living part of some four-faceted being, an octopus with people for its tentacles.

The chapters where all this takes place—chapters 2 to 9 in the third book of the first part, which is entitled "In the

Year 1817"—are preceded by a further dizzying as well as lighthearted chronicle of the main events of that year, which creates an appropriate setting for the action. Then the two collective characters take center stage, the bohemian students and their female conquests, who are abandoned at the end of the evening's entertainment.

The revolutionary students of the ABC that Marius joins when he leaves his grandfather's house also function as a collective character, especially at the outset, when it is very difficult to tell them apart. Enjolras, Combeferre, Jean Prouvaire, Feuilly, Courfeyrac, Bahorel, Lesgle or Laigle, Joly, and Grantaire are, until the moment of the barricade, little more than one being with many faces, rebellious young men from the Midi (the one exception is Laigle), now resident in Paris, where they observe the same rituals and have the same habits. At the beginning, readers struggle to work out what is individual to each of these characters apart from their names. We soon realize that this is a futile endeavor, because though they seem to be different individuals, they are in fact the same person spread across different dialogues and actions. It is only later, at the testing moment of the barricade, when the collective character becomes more diversified and hierarchical, that rather more individual types begin to emerge. These range between the extremes of the republican radical leader Enjolras, who is full of ideas and ideals, and the drunken Grantaire, a pessimist and a cynic, who gets himself killed alongside Enjolras out of friendship.

Another important collective character in *Les Misérables*, although its presence is less pronounced than these earlier examples—which is natural, because the people who belong to it rank among the "shady," sinister characters—is the Patron-Minette gang. Babet, Guelemer, Claquesous,

Jondrette, and Montparnasse, whom the Thénardiers recruit for the ambush in the Gorbeau tenement, cause a shiver of terror every time they appear, always in the shadows, as if they have just emerged from hell, because their mere presence, their evil ferocity, reeking of prison and recent crimes, is a portent of further bloodshed and criminality. We scarcely hear their voices; we barely see their outline in the shadows they inhabit, as if the light of day might dissolve them. They always go round in a group, for it seems that, even though they are now free, they are still joined by the chain gang. The chain gang—where they first met, and which will be their ultimate fate—has fashioned them into a malevolent brotherhood, turning them into human vermin with five heads, ten feet, and ten arms.

Other collective characters are more fleeting and ephemeral, like the men in prison with Jean Valjean in Toulon, Brevet, Chenildieu, and Cochepaille, the nuns at Petit Picpus, the soldiers at Waterloo, the national guard that stamp out the Paris insurrection, and the crowds celebrating carnival in the streets on the day that Marius and Cosette get married. They all form a living backcloth, a chorus, in front of which the heroes of the story play out their roles, be they admirable, appalling, or mediocre. Playing a part: in this novel, this is a synonym of living. For in the novel, life is a great theater, and the characters—good and evil, godlike or insignificant, shadowy or luminous—are all magnificent actors.

CHAPTER IV

# The Great Theater of the World

The hero of *Les Misérables* is called Jean Valjean, but in prison, on account of his exceptional strength, the other prisoners rebaptized him Jean Le Cric, while to the wardens he was just a number, first 24601 and later 9430. This instability in names even precedes the birth of Victor Hugo's hero, because the father of this peasant from Brie was probably not called Valjean, but Vlajean, which might have been a nickname, a contraction of *Voilà-Jean*, Here's Jean! (I, II, VI, p. 88).

Once free, Jean Valjean will become Monsieur Madeleine, a prosperous industrialist and the mayor of Montreuil-sur-mer. In Paris, he will be the rentier Monsieur Leblanc, Urbain Fabre, and, in the convent of Petit-Picpus, Ultime Fauchelevent or simply, "the other Fauchelevent," as the nuns call him. The play on Jean Valjean's names does not end here, because at various points in the story—this happens to other characters as well—the narrator decides to make him anonymous and, as if he means to shuffle the identities of his characters, starts calling him, enigmatically, "the man," "the person," "the human being." This happens on several occasions, for example, in book 3 of the second part, "Fulfillment of the Promise Made to the Dead Woman," the chapters that narrate Cosette's meeting with a stranger in the darkness of the woods. This man helps her carry her bucket of water and later rescues her from the clutches of the Thénardiers. The narrator rather naively hides from us the identity of Jean Valjean, since we recognize him immediately. And as if the names he invents for himself were not enough, other people give him different names. When the inhabitants of Montreuil-sur-mer find out that Monsieur Madeleine is a former galley slave, they gossip that his real name is "horrible: something like Béjean, Bojean, or Boujean" (I, VIII, V, p. 309).

It has been argued that this proliferation of names is caused by poverty, which strips the characters of "what society guarantees for other people: individuality, a language, a conscience, a personal history, an identity."[1] Yet these changes are more than an illustration of social protest. With these games, the narrator is looking not to deceive us, but rather, by using the conventions of the stage, to emphasize the theatrical nature of the story that he is telling, the performance that is *Les Misérables*. Life in the novel is theatrical, and the characters are actors who follow the melodramatic script and frequently change appearance— change names—as so often happens above all in the farces of popular theater.

In an essay entitled "*Les Misérables*: Théâtre-Roman,"[2] Anne Ubersfeld points out that Victor Hugo began to take notes for *Les Misérables* at a time when he had put to one side his draft of the play *Les Jumeaux* (The Twins), and that he began to write the text almost immediately after the failure of his play *Les Burgraves*.[3] Hugo wrote the novel when he had not completely given up working as a dramatist, and it is plausible that the conception and the techniques of the genre might have found their way surreptitiously into the fiction he was writing, making it theatrical from the outset. For theater is indeed central to the novel, to its plot, and to the spaces inhabited by its characters, particular *les misérables* of the story, like Gavroche, the Thénardiers, and the ruffians from Patron-Minette. It can also be seen in the way the story is presented and in the behavior—the self-assuredness, the gestures, and the speeches—of the characters. For Anne Ubersfeld, Gavroche—who is called Grimebodin and then Chavroche before he is given a permanent name—is the most theatrical character in the novel, not because his behavior is particularly histrionic but because the urchin always goes to the theater, through the side door, and has contact with a theater company, who give him tickets. She also points out that almost all the Patron-Minette gang—Babet, Guelemer, and Claquesous (who calls himself Pas du Tout, and, on the barricade, Le Cabuc)—are, or have been, linked to boulevard theater, as clowns, comics, or bit actors in melodramas. It is certainly true that the novel reveals "a theatricality in the lower depths, a social theater of crime, a carnival of horror" (p. 124).

## Adjectives to Describe the Show

In a dossier he wrote for *Les Misérables*, Hugo was found to have listed a series of adjectives: "*Étonnant, extraordinaire, surprenant, surhumain, surnaturel, inouï, fauve, sinistre, formidable, gigantesque, sauvage, colossal, monstreux, difforme, effaré, frissonnant, lugubre, funèbre, hideux, épouvantable, téné-*

*breux, mystérieux, fantastique, nocturne, crépusculaire.*"[4] These were not adjectives picked by chance, for stylistic purposes, but rather they were meant to determine the mood of the story. And there is no doubt that he succeeded in his objective, because all these adjectives perfectly suit his operatic novel.[5] None of these adjectives allude to realism, to a representation that reproduces the everyday world that is easily identifiable to the reader. They all refer to "another" world, of excess, extravagance, surprise, and color. A world that could be found in the most gruesome melodramas of popular theater. This world had moved from the stage to the serial novel, and was depicted in that most successful of all serial novels, Eugène Sue's *Les Mystères de Paris* (which was published between 19 June 1842 and 15 October 1843 in *Le Journal des Débats*). This was a novel that Victor Hugo read with enthusiasm, and which he would later cannibalize to good effect in his masterpiece.

If we reread this list of adjectives, we see that almost every one of them seems to define one of the evil characters in the novel: the *ténébreux* Thénardier, the innkeeper, a ruffian, an exploiter, and an innate criminal, who tends to appear in the night rather than in the day because he feels an irresistible attraction for the shadows, for a life of stealth. After Jean Valjean, he is the character whose name changes most often. He is Thénardier in Montfermeil, and in Paris he is called Jondrette, the name he uses for his criminal activities. When he writes his begging letters, passing himself off as an actor or a man of letters, he disguises himself with the names Genflot and Fabantou. Javert, by contrast, has only one name—he has no surname—but that does not make him any less theatrical (although he is more tempered in his speech) than the other characters. We see him disguised as a church beggar to spy on the ex-convict, and, in an extreme histrionic gesture, he asks Jean Valjean for money, which Valjean gives him. The names of the Thénardiers' daughters are not stable either. The younger daughter was baptized Gulnare but ends up being called Azelma; the elder, Éponine, is called Ponine by Cosette.

As a young girl Fantine was called La Blonde because of her "sun-colored" hair, and the real name of the daughter of Fantine and Tholomyès is Euphrasie, but her mother calls her Cosette and this sticks. In Montfermeil they call her The Lark. Before he gets to know her, Marius imagines that she is called Ursule. Madame Thénardier used to call her "unnamed dog" or "the other," little knowing that the orphan girl whom she despises and exploits will, through marriage, gain a surname and also the title of Baroness Pontmercy. But this continual changing of names—disguises, masks—is not the only theatrical feature of the characters. They also, on occasion, without changing names, play different roles. Marius, as a young man, is a supporter of the Bourbons, a monarchist, like his grandfather, but when he claims his father's heritage, he becomes a Bonapartist and a steadfast defender of the empire. The same thing happens to Cosette who, as a child, is very different from the young woman who, after five years in the convent of Petit-Picpus, rejoins society as a bourgeois young lady, without any mystery or spark to her. One might even say that she is completely soulless, because she is so insipid and because she accepts life with a resigned indifference. Out of all these role changes, one of the most remarkable is that of Monsieur Mabeuf, the ex-treasurer of the Church of Saint Suplice, the tenderhearted amateur botanist, who loves his plants and is a good and peaceful man. After he falls into the most abject poverty, we see him

on the barricade at La Chanvrerie, where he is taken for a
"representative of the people" and a "regicide," and where
he will die a hero's death.

## Performance, Beauty, and Life

All these changes of name, nicknames, disguises, parts, and
performances, this sense of acting rather than living—of
living to act—are primarily a result of the characters' subordination to the narrator of *Les Misérables*. He is the director of the show, and his invasive personality sucks the independence out of his characters, turning them into puppets
whose strings he can move at will. The narrator is the only
completely free person in this world, the only person with
an unfettered free will. The characters, whom he kills off
and resurrects at will, are all confined, because, like actors,
they have to keep to a script, to perform actions and dialogues that have been rigorously assigned to them, and
which they must act out under the unflagging gaze of the
narrator. At the first signs of unrest from the characters,
the narrator comes forward and moves them off the stage,
monopolizing the action himself.

This relationship between the divine stenographer and
the characters in *Les Misérables* brings to mind the relationship that Calderón de la Barca established between the Author and his creations in one of his most famous *autos sac-
ramentales* (allegorical religious plays), *El gran teatro del
mundo* (The Great Theater of the World), which he must
have written, according to the critics, around 1635. And
this is not the only similarity between the two works. The
Calderonian drama is an allegory of human fate, or history,
conceived as a theatrical farce, a dramatic simulacrum of

real life, which is not the life of the body but that of the soul. The World makes this point very precisely:

> Pass from truth to the theater
> Because this theater is the place of fictions.[6]

Life is a fiction: only after death will human beings attain real life. Life on earth is a play in which each man and each woman is given a part by the Author, on whom they all depend, as slaves depend on their masters. The Author of Calderón's *auto sacramental* has the same overwhelming, asphyxiating, total control over his creations as the narrator in *Les Misérables*, and the freedom that the characters enjoy in the novel is identical to that of those actors on the stage: the course of their lives—their beginning and their end and their journey from the cradle to the grave—is mapped out in an inflexible and inevitable way. The characters in the novel could say to the divine stenographer what, in the name of his subjects, the King says to the Author in *El gran teatro del mundo*:

> We have no soul, senses, power,
> Life or reason.
> We are formless,
> We are dust at your feet.
> Blow this dust, then,
> So that we may act.

However, when they interpret their role, these slaves have a margin for initiative, improvisation, and innovation that, at times, might almost be mistaken for free will. This leads the audience to believe that since they are playing their parts so well, with such understanding and conviction, they are not acting but living, and their life is thus not subject to the dictates of a script, but enjoys the risks and the uncertainties of people who are free and can decide their actions for themselves. Just as we find in *El gran teatro del mundo*, in Victor Hugo's novel, no matter how lavish and spectacular the performance, the primordial reality, the underlying drama, is to be found not in the precarious life of the flesh and human behavior, but in the other life, which is invisible and eternal, that precedes and continues after the performance.

As in the theater or in the cinema, the actors in *Les Misérables* do not always seem to be manipulated by the narrator. It depends on the parts they are playing. Some, like Gavroche, for example, are rebellious and seem to act with a spontaneity that the others lack. But it also depends on their acting skills, on how well they can play their part. They all have some talent as actors, and some, like the comedian in the novel, Monsieur Gillenormand, have a great deal of talent, because he moves effortlessly in the world of farce, caricature, and excess that the narrator has invented for him.

The theatricality of the characters—of the world of *Les Misérables*—can also be seen in the way they speak, in the peculiar nature of the dialogues. The use of language is skillfully designed to free the novel from real reality and turn it into fictive reality. The narrator and his creatures are always looking for emotional impact. They are full of grand gestures. Like orators seeking applause, they use dramatic phrases to round off their long speeches. They start out addressing someone but soon forget their interlocutors, taking over the stage for themselves. Some of these monologues start out as dialogues but then change into soliloquies in which the characters step off the stage and address the audience directly.

Excess is always the hallmark of their performance. The situations are exaggerated to the point of almost undermining the credibility of the narrative. However, the director is skillful enough to be able to restrain and moderate this excess whenever it looks like falling into caricature. In fact, the reality of the novel, like that of a play, is an independent reality. By cleverly manipulating and organizing the components of reality, the narrator has built another reality.

This desire for effect through posturing or unusual behavior can be seen in many instances in the novel. What could be more theatrical than the death of the bohemian Grantaire, who, while his companions are preparing to fight and die for their ideals, gets happily drunk, quite impervious to what is going on around him. However, when he comes round in an alcoholic daze, he shows not the least compunction in being shot alongside Enjolras, the friend he idolizes. All the deaths in the novel are theatrical: some are cinematographic, like those of Gavroche, Monsieur Mabuse, and Enjolras on the barricade; others follow the pattern of classic tragedy, like that of Fantine in the Hospital de Montreuil-sur-mer, or Jean Valjean's death in the little house on the Rue de L'Homme-Armé. Javert's death is also tragic—out of Racine—as he plunges into the watery depths of the rapid-flowing Seine. Although somewhat less showy, the death of G, the former member of the Convention, has an operatic tinge. According to Bernard Leuilliot, it reworks "the death of Socrates": he is dying at sunset with the cold invading his body and numbing his limbs until it reaches his heart, at which moment the young country boy arrives "to help his master the way that Socrates' disciples assisted him."[7]

## Light and Shadow

It is not just human beings that are "luminous" or "shadowy"; events also take place either in the light or in the shadows. The choice is not accidental, but rather follows a strict dramatic order. In the daylight, love can blossom, beauty can be contemplated, as in the Jardin de Luxembourg where Marius, in love, goes to gaze on Cosette. The darkness is the place where the Patron-Minette bandits plan their escapes, their ambushes, and their crimes.

The semidarkness, the failing light, the fading outlines and silhouettes, and the onset of the night: this is the time for mystery, strange meetings, visions, nightmares, surprises, and revelations. One of the most unforgettable scenes in the novel comes just before Jean Valjean rescues Cosette from the Thénardiers. The entire sequence takes place at nightfall. We see the cruelty of the couple, who turn on the girl whom they exploit and abuse—she is dressed in rags and has one eye swollen from a blow from the innkeeper's wife—and force her to fetch water from a wood that is now in semidarkness. As the girl, doubled over by the weight of the bucket and frightened to death, struggles along almost blindly, her freedom arrives in the form of an anonymous giant who, without saying a word, takes the bucket and puts his hand on her shoulders, a promise of safety and love that will radically change her destiny. This slow and ceremonious scene, which contains all the ingredients of the romantic serial novel, manages, through the expert handling of these ingredients, to touch us and have us suspend our critical judgment.

## Sets

The locations where the action takes place are also theatrical, because they frequently seem like sets, artificial constructions installed in the novel to reinforce symbolically, through their strange and appealing design, a sense of being in another world, another reality, a fictional place. One striking example is the great Elephant in the Bastille that the Paris urchin, through his inventiveness and imagination, has turned into his residence. Gavroche changes the function of the enormous Elephant, turning the extravagant monument into an eccentric dwelling and hideout. He has fashioned out of the metal and wooden entrails of the trunk a secret nest that protects him against the rain and the storms, but where he must remain constantly alert, keeping at bay the armies of rats that, like him, have taken over the space.

And is the Gorbeau tenement, with its dilapidated, labyrinthine structure, full of marginal and poor people, any less theatrical than the Elephant of the Bastille? There, in that lugubrious, shadowy, mysterious place where—in accordance with the law of the irresistible traps—Jean Valjean and Cosette, Marius, Thénardier, and Javert all meet, the most theatrical episode of the novel takes place. Here, as in gothic stories or in Grand Guignol, we witness the fake Monsieur Leblanc, who has been kidnapped by Thénardier and the Patron-Minette gang, anticipating the tortures that his kidnappers are threatening him with by burning his own arm with a red-hot iron. This disturbing, exaggerated scene seems aimed at surprising and affecting not the villains so much as the invisible people sitting behind Thénardier and his accomplices, who are watching the performance from another reality: we the readers are the intended audience for this proud, self-assured gesture.

## The Victor at Waterloo

It is not surprising, therefore, that in such a histrionic and theatrical world, the narrator can claim with total conviction that "[t]he man who won the Battle of Waterloo was not the defeated Napoleon, or Wellington, who was giving way at four o'clock and was desperate at five, or Blücher, who scarcely fought; the man who won the Battle of Waterloo was Cambronne" (II, I, XV, p. 356). Cambronne, the "little-known officer," was in charge of one of the "squares" of the imperial guard, and he kept fighting back at the enemy artillery even though defeat was inevitable and his force was being decimated. Exhorted by one of the English generals, Colville or Maitland, to save his life and his men by surrendering, Cambronne answers, *Merde!* (II, I, XIV, p. 356). The author of this response—a gesture, a word—was the true hero of the carnage that sealed the fate of Napoleon and the empire because, as the divine stenographer explains, "[t]o smite the thunder that kills you with such a word is to be victorious" (II, I, XV, p. 356). Cambronne's excremental oath soars out of history into the timeless space of myth, as a symbol, an image that encapsulates all the beauty and loftiness of that historical tragedy. For this reason, the furious *Merde!*[8] is "perhaps the most beautiful word ever uttered by a Frenchman" (II, I, XV, p. 356). As in theater, as in art, it is the forms that create the contents, which give life and history their meaning.

## Human Putrefaction

This *merde* that Victor Hugo placed so boldly in his novel, provoking the anger of many high-minded critics, is more than just an exclamation that expresses the courage, honor, and heroism of a little-known military officer who, by proclaiming the word, gains in stature and becomes immortal. It is also a substance that imposes its filthy and pestilential

THE GREAT THEATER OF THE WORLD 99

reality on a central aspect of existence; it is a component of the shadows and the underground, that nightmarish, noxious-smelling set where the "darkest" episode in the novel takes place.

Perhaps the most spectacular setting in this performance is "the Entrails of the Leviathan," the labyrinthine sewers of Paris that Jean Valjean stumbles through with Marius on his back, sinking in the mire, lost in the darkness, risking his life a thousand times, almost hopeless, but never wavering, drawing strength from that desire to do good which, for Jean Valjean, is so bound up with a desire to atone and to punish himself. These foul-smelling shadows, where the waste, the rubbish, and the excrescencies of the great city pile up on the slippery, suppurating stone passageways, are a dung heap, a metaphor, a prefiguration of hell, a horrific underworld in which the devil Thénardier moves as freely as if he were in his own home.

When, just before the fall of the barricade at La Chanvrerie, Jean Valjean plunges underground with the unconscious Marius on his back, the action makes one of its typical pauses. The narrator embarks on an unexpected soliloquy during which, quite forgetting the plot, he spends six chapters literally dragging the reader through excrement that is much thicker, more extensive, and more noxious than the verbal and metaphorical *merde* that Cambronne hurls at his English adversary at Waterloo: the excrement piled up in the forty leagues of the entrails of Paris. These are extraordinary pages. They begin with an enthusiastic scientific description of the virtues of excrement as a fertilizer to enrich the land, and of the material gain that a good government can extract from this human waste.[9] They then gradually turn into a detailed examination of the sewers and waste pipes of the city, which offer a grandiose mirror that reflects the abject state of life itself: "the history of mankind is reflected in the history of its cloaca" (V, II, II, p. 1285). There is a very detailed description of the different phases in the construction of this network of passages, channels, pits, and caves that receives, stores, and evacuates a putrefaction that is not just material and physical, but also moral and metaphysical. "The sewer is the conscience of the city"; "the sewer is a cynic who tells all," because in the sewers, "through which history flows," we find "a sincerity of filth" and we breathe in "the huge miasma of social catastrophes" (V, II, II, pp. 1286–1287). The examples pile up, gleaned over the centuries from the ancient cities of the Far East and from the Bible, from the Middle Ages and from the history of Paris. In an adventurous voyage worthy of Homeric heroes or discoverers of oceans and continents, a civic hero explores the pestilential entrails of Paris for seven years, between 1805 and 1812, a man whom the narrator compares to the great Napoleonic generals. He is called Bruneseau, the inspector general of health under the empire, whose reports on his exploration of the sewers Victor Hugo consulted, along with other documents, when he came to write "The Entrails of the Leviathan."

When the divine stenographer takes up the plot once again and we see Jean Valjean begin his journey, dragging the inert body of Marius along like a cross, through the sewers of Paris, the setting that he enters is no longer part of the same reality in which the rebellion and the fall of the barricade in La Chanvrerie have just taken place. The evil-smelling shadows that he stumbles through, among rotting substances, fetid remains, vermin, and putrefaction, are at once the waste matter of Paris and also the "lower" human regions that Mikhail Bakhtin talks about in his study of Rabelais,[10] that dirty human terrain where life is composed of urine and shit, where filth and viscous materials accumulate, the poisons that the organism must expel so that it does not rot.[11] The journey of the ex-convict through the sewers of Paris is both a physical journey and also a rite of passage, in search of a way out that will guarantee his material survival and also his spiritual health, his redemption. The interminable, somnambulist, way of the cross followed by Jean Valjean and his human burden is the culmination, in the final pages of the novel, of his lengthy penance, of a life spent expiating a distant wrongdoing through indescribable sacrifice. The fact that, at the end of this supreme test, Jean Valjean manages to find the way out seals his final redemption. He has passed the test; he has emerged victorious from the battle against the darkness, the filth, the carrion. To a certain extent, he has freed himself from evil. That is why, when the ex-convict finally sees the way out, "He stood upright, shivering, frozen, foul, bent over by the weight of the dying man whom he had been carrying, dripping with mire, and *with his soul filled with a strange clarity*" (V, III, V, p. 1322, my emphasis). Immediately afterward, the secret vein of destiny rewards him, freeing him of Javert as well, that enemy who, like a bad conscience, had pursued him implacably for so many years.

Although less obviously showy and vivid than the monumentally theatrical episode "The Entrails of the Leviathan," almost all the other settings in the novel are very closely related to the actions that take place within them. This is true of the barricade of La Chanvrerie, the convent of Petit-Picpus, that sanctuary outside time and history, the solitary tavern run by the Thénardiers in Montfermeil, Monsieur Mabuse's very modest dwelling, bursting with plants and exotic flowers, the garden in the Rue Plumet, with its tangled, richly scented undergrowth, which eavesdrops on the words of love spoken by Marius and Cosette, and it is true even of Monseigneur Myriel's modest house in Digne. Characters, objects, and landscapes are not "real" in *Les Misérables*: they are part of the fiction; they are themselves fictional. But their artifice is not divorced from life. Instead, as happens when successful works are staged, this artifice presents a simulacrum that is so coherent, convincing, and genuine that it persuades us to take it for real life.

## *Life as Fiction*

This is the context in which we must see the play on names in the novel. There is no doubt that by juggling the names and playing games with the identities of his characters, the narrator is looking to subvert our expectations, disorienting us and then surprising us by stripping off a character's mask to reveal someone whom we have already come across in the fiction. Beneath these conscious—technical—intentions there is something much deeper that has to do with the nature of fictive reality. Here the identities of men and women are changeable, and transitory, so fleeting and fickle that, strictly speaking, they do not exist. Or rather, they exist only in the transitory identities that the actors assume when they tread the boards to give life to the heroes of fiction. Human beings have not *one* identity—an essence—but several. They have provisional lives, and circumstances impose on them certain roles that have assigned to them specific names (a specific mask).

The scene in which this transient nature of human identity—the disguises that cover an essential void—is symbolically represented is "L'affaire Champmathieu," a trial that sets out to verify a man's identity. Is the poor man standing before the court Jean Valjean, or isn't he? It is not just the judges and the authorities and the spectators packing into the court who are inclined to believe that he is Valjean, owing to the weight of evidence brought by the police to prove their case. Even Jean Valjean himself is not sure. When he enters the courtroom in Arras, he thinks that he is seeing double, and, in a dream, he sees himself sitting on the bench, coming to life in the figure of Champmathieu: "He had, before his eyes, a strange vision, a sort of representation of the most horrible moment of his life, interpreted by a ghost" (I, VII, IX, p. 278). The truth is that if Jean Valjean had not overcome the wrenching anguish that had tormented him throughout the whole evening, and had not faced the court, giving concrete proof that he was the man whom they were looking for, then poor old Champmathieu would have been punished in his place—his name and person substituted for another's—and he would have become Jean Valjean to all intents and purposes.

This ambiguity can be seen in many instances. Just because Marius's father, Colonel Pontmercy, mistakenly believed that Thénardier, the jackal of Waterloo, had saved his life, Marius must express his gratitude and feel indebted for this generous act, an act that never took place because Thénardier was on the battlefield (at night, of course) only to steal from the corpses. The characters in the novel never clear up this misunderstanding, and both Marius and his father have an idea of Thénardier that is a fiction within the fiction.

Novels, great novels in particular, are not testimonies or documents of life itself. They offer another life, endowed with its own attributes, that is created to discredit real life.

They hold up a mirror that seems to reflect real life but in fact deforms real life, adds fresh touches, reshapes it. As Anne Ubersfeld argues, *Les Misérables* "constructs a parallel universe, that makes no pretense of being referential reality; it creates an imaginary space in which the word 'theatrical' can be heard as a playful word, a word of desire."[12]

What an extraordinary performance this is, that through the coherence of its structure and the subtle distance it keeps from the reality it purports to describe, fiction can free itself from reality and offer an image that is a negation of this reality. And what an excessive performance it is, so ambitious that it seeks to embrace the whole of its time, the entire history and society of its day. Through this all-encompassing vision, which includes the main characters and the extras, the choruses, the collective characters that are bound up in the play, we are presented with the dizzying illusion that *Les Misérables*, the Great Theater of the World, is an artificial, magical, and all-embracing object like Borges's Aleph, in which is contained all the experiences, the adventures and the misfortunes, the pettiness and the greatness, of the human adventure.[13]

# CHAPTER V

# Rich, Poor, Leisured, Idle, and Marginal

In a treatise on prostitution that was going to appear in the third part of *Les Misérables*, but was eventually left out of the final manuscript, the divine stenographer distinguishes between history, which is the responsibility of men and women, and fate, which human beings have to accept with resignation since they have no power over it: "The portion of fate that depends on man is called 'Misère,' and it can be abolished. The portion of fate that depends on the unknown is called 'Douleur,' and this must be considered and explored with trepidation. Let us improve what we can and accept the rest."[1] In other words, social injustices—ignorance, poverty, exploitation, miscarriages of justice—are attributable to men and women and can disappear or improve with better governance of society. But even if injustices disappear, a degree of suffering will still be allotted to each individual, and, since we can do nothing about this destiny, we must accept that it is part of the human condition. This statement anticipated by a century the distinction that Camus would make between history, over which men and women have total control, and metaphysics, where the fate of the human being is irreversible. Ontological pessimism and historical optimism are the main philosophical tenets of the novel, the narrator of *Les Misérables* declares whenever he philosophizes about injustice and destiny, which he does on numerous occasions. Do the events in the novel confirm this philosophy? Can one see the division between them in the characters' lives? For some characters, like Jean Valjean and Gavroche, it is clear which misfortunes befall them as a consequence of an unjust society and which are due to an ineluctable design. In the case of other characters, like Éponine, this dividing line disappears. The unhappiness of this young woman is due as much to the fact that she is the daughter of a bandit and an inhuman father as to the fact that she is in love with Marius, who does not love her, or even notice her love for him. In so many of the characters, like Éponine, the individual and the social are intertwined to such an extent that it is impossible to tell whether their happiness or misfortune is due to the ills of society or to unfathomable divine will. In any event, the depiction of human problems, history, and the human condition is a lot less schematic than the statements by the narrator would have us believe. Just as life is always richer than the theories that attempt to explain it, a story is always something more than a mere illustration of the narrator's theories.

In the brief epigraph to *Les Misérables*, signed in Hauteville House on 1 January 1862, which he used in place of the "Philosophical Preface," Victor Hugo states that the intention of the novel is to denounce, and help to remedy, social injustice: ". . . while ignorance and poverty remain on this earth, books such as this cannot be completely useless." These lines are suffused with optimism. Literature can fight against social injustice; it can help to improve history; it is an arm of Progress that the author believes in blindly. However, the Victor Hugo who finishes the novel in 1860–1862 is not the same person who had begun it in 1845, or had worked on it for a time in 1851. Unlike writers who start out as revolutionaries and end up as reactionaries, he, as a young man, was a monarchist, a Bourbon, and a *Vendéen*, like his mother, then an Orleanist during the reign of Louis-Philippe. In later years he was a liberal and a republican, and, at the time of the Commune, he articulated somewhat hazy socialist and anarchist ideas. Was this a natural evolution, or was it dictated by convenience? Until the rise to power of Louis Bonaparte, whom he opposed, and in particular after the coup of 2 December 1851, the changes that occur in the great writer's political ideas could be seen as opportunistic because they coincide with changes in the power elite and they earn him honors and favors. Even taking into account his opposition to Louis Bonaparte in the Assembly—1850–1851—at a time when the government was moving to the right and becoming militaristic, a period when his behavior is visibly governed by conviction, Hugo's political views have always seemed to me somewhat dubious, as can be seen in a note written in September 1848, when he outlines a chameleon philosophical stance: "I am red with the reds, white with the whites, and blue with the blues. In other words, I am for the people, for order, and for freedom."[2]

Exile played a decisive role in his ideological evolution and saved the writer from the public figure because, in 1851, Victor Hugo seemed to be suffocating under the weight of his social and academic life, his erotic adventures and his political activities. Exile makes him take up liberal and radical positions, and this transformation can be seen throughout *Les Misérables*. For that reason, his way of conceiving France's political and social problems—his idea of history—changes radically between the first and second versions of the novel. He was quite aware of this fact, as can be seen in a note to remind himself that he must change Marius's political opinions so they chime with his new political point of view: "Reform all Marius's Bonapartism and make him democratic and liberal."[3] He also suppressed, in the 1860–1862 version, a long text entitled "Some Pages of History," which he had written in 1848, and which was initially to be included at the beginning of the fourth part of the novel, because in it he had argued that a republic was not suitable for France.[4]

In the novel, Monsieur Gillenormand's grandson has an ideological evolution similar to that experienced by Victor Hugo. And at some point during the second revision of *Les Misérables*, Hugo felt it necessary to explain the changes in his political outlook within the text itself (although he would later leave out this passage), confessing that he had been "illogical and honest, a legitimist and a Voltairean, a literary Christian, a liberal Bonapartist, a tentative royalist socialist." He added that he held these opinions in good faith and that, "in everything that I have written, you will never find a single line against freedom."[5]

This biographical digression is not gratuitous, because the political changes that the author went through in the years when he was writing the novel have a bearing—in the case of Marius very explicitly—on certain contradictions and the often hazy sociopolitical content of the novel. How could the vague reformist idealism of *Les Misérables* have been seen by so many critics of the time as inflammatory and subversive? Because the reactions of Narciso Gay, quoted in the first chapter, and those of the Spanish bishops who had the book burned, were not the only trenchant statements made against what was to many a corrosive, immoral book that threatened public order. And a great number of readers agreed with Barbey D'Aurevilly that the intention of the novel was to "blow up all the institutions of society, one after the other, with something more deadly than cannon fire that can shake mountains: with tears and with devotion."[6]

How times have changed, or, rather, how right-wing positions have softened, while left-wing positions have become more extreme. Because, in its analysis of social problems, this subversive, horrifying book does not go any further than recognizing that society is imperfect because "[t]he saintly law of Jesus Christ governs our civilization but has not yet permeated this civilization" (I, V, XI, p. 180). The result is that we find material and moral destitution, aberrations like the death penalty, an inhuman judicial and penal system, and immense religious, moral, and social prejudices. All this must be reformed, of course, and sooner or later it will be, because Progress is the inevitable destiny of human civilization. What will destroy destitution? Teaching, education, schools. What will end poverty? Charity, solidarity, a spirit of justice, and the development of science. In the society of the future, imbued with an authentic Christian spirit, the poor will have disappeared—not the rich—along with prejudice and capital punishment, and the prisons will have been reformed. Everyone will have access to schooling, and the culture learned in the classroom will bring to an end this dark night of error and horror in the history of man. For "the true division in humanity is between those who live in light and those who live in darkness. The aim is to reduce the number of those who live in darkness and increase the number of those who live in the light. That is why we cry: Education! Knowledge! To learn to read is to light a fire; every syllable spelled out is a spark" (I, V, VII, I, p. 1009). What so infuriated conservatives of the time was not an anarchist or a socialist book, but a book that was timidly liberal and social democratic.

## Reformist Idealism

The theorists of this future society that would come about, sooner or later, with the development of history, are the two most political characters in the novel: the Conventionist G and Enjolras. Victor Hugo made the first of these characters his mouthpiece. He imbued him with his own ideas about the inevitability of progress, God as the motor force of history, and his conviction that, despite the excesses of '93, the French Revolution was the most important event in human history. The character is profoundly romantic: he is a social pariah, an individual whom the people of Digne view with "a kind of horror" and treat as an outcast. What crime has this old man, whom the narrator refers to just as G, committed? He was a member of the Convention, the regicidal institution that in January 1793 approved the death sentence for Louis XVI (although G voted against it, because of his opposition to the death penalty). In this small Alpine province in Restoration France, this man represents all the abominations of the Revolution, and the parishioners of Monseigneur Bienvenu regard him with mistrust and disgust, as a kind of wild beast. This attitude is dictated by ignorance, prejudice, and stupidity, characteristics that, in *Les Misérables*, belong to collective groups, to social organizations, rather than to individuals.

In fact, G the Conventionist is an upright, honest, idealistic, generous, and profoundly ethical man, a lay saint—another one of the just—as Monseigneur Myriel discovers during their long conversation. The whole chapter, "The Bishop in the Presence of a Strange Light" (I, I, X), added in 1861 during Hugo's exile in Jersey, and the subject of ferocious attacks from conservative critics, reveals a deep affinity between the two seemingly irreconcilable men, the revolutionary and the bishop, a shared set of feelings, codes of conduct, social ideas, and even beliefs. What was to be a confrontation turns into an almost complete identification between the two men, as Monseigneur Bienvenu understands when he is filled by the "strange light" that emanates from the old man, and ends up asking for his blessing. In fact, there is nothing in G's ideological viewpoint to worry the bishop. The old man believes in God and in "the advance of mankind toward the light"; he thinks that revolutions are part of the price that has to be paid for the progressive amelioration of society—which he refers to, in a striking image, as "the brutalities of progress"—and that the Revolution has been "the greatest step forward by mankind since the coming of Christ." He does not excuse the excesses of '93, but he explains them as the consequence of injustices accumulated over centuries of social neglect. Like the narrator, like Victor Hugo, G believes that culture will eradicate injustice because the greatest human tyranny is ignorance. Man's conscience is the "amount of inner knowledge that we possess."

This optimistic, idealist view of the destiny of human history is not essentially different from that expressed by the revolutionary Enjolras, who dramatically outlines his vision of the future in a speech to his insurrectionary comrades, delivered on the top of the barricade, just before his death. This text, like all of the fifth part of the novel, was added in 1860–1862 and comes in a chapter entitled significantly "What Can Be Seen from the Top of the Barricade" (V, I, V). Faith in progress, a conviction that society in the future will achieve individual liberty along with social justice, a belief that the advance of science—the truth of science—will help to foster truth and morality in men and society: these are the foundations of the young man's ideology. Man has "tamed matter," for the hydra of the ancients is now called a steamship, the dragon is called the locomotive, and the griffin is known as the balloon. All that remains is for man to "achieve the ideal" (identical to the ideal promoted by Saint-Simon and his followers: that science would become enshrined in government): "reality governed by truth, that is our aim." The nineteenth century has made these scientific advances, and it would be up to the twentieth century to undertake the grandiose task of making happiness a reality, in a society that Enjolras describes in lavish detail: "City streets bathed in light, green branches on the thresholds of houses, all nations sisters, all men just; old men blessing children, the past loving the present, thinkers enjoying complete freedom and religious believers enjoying equality, heaven itself is religion, God is the direct priest and the human conscience is an altar, no more hatred, fraternity in workshops and in schools, notoriety both punishment and reward, work for all, justice for all, and peace, no more bloodshed and war" (V, I, V p. 1213).

Since the twentieth century did not live up to Enjolras's predictions, and since, with all its apocalyptic events, its conflicts, the increase in economic and social inequality among individuals, classes, and nations, and the onset of crises of every shape and form, this century did not justify the hopes and visions of the old Conventionist and the young rebel, their ideas can be seen to have a poetic, rather than a historical, density. They are a utopia that contains the "added element" of the fictive reality. Since the publication of *Les Misérables*, real reality has given the lie, on innumerable occasions, to the belief that culture is the enemy of barbarism—a cultured Germany adopted Nazism and carried out the genocide of six million Jews—and it is now difficult to argue that advances in science are accompanied by a simultaneous advance in moral truth. Quite the reverse, scientific development in the twentieth century often shored up tyrannical and imperialist regimes that stifled any form of freedom within, and engaged in naked colonialism and imperialism, exploiting and plundering poor countries. In an era in which international divisions are multiplying, in which local conflicts throw up daily enormous numbers of casualties, and in which societies in the first and third worlds are devastated by repression and terrorism, unemployment and inflation, corruption and tyranny, the liberal, scientific utopianism found in *Les Misérables*, so much at odds with the reality of readers today, helps to make the book seem, in ideological terms, a work of the past, whose charm lies in its being an elegant, anachronistic curiosity, like an old almanac. It is for the same reason that *Madame Bovary* and *L'Éducation Sentimentale*, which are so imbued with Flaubert's political and social pessimism, seem today agonizingly modern and extremely realistic. Its ideology—its vision of history and society— offers another proof that *Les Misérables* is a fiction, a creation that turns its back on lived experience, a mirage created through the radical transformation of the real reality of people and events. Like the characters and the plot of the novel, its political and social vision is essentially an invention.

## The Just

While G the Conventionist and Enjolras philosophize about the future and act within organized groups—assemblies, parties, societies—to change the present, other characters in the novel also fight against social injustice, but in an individual manner, motivated not by theories, by ideology, but by noble feelings and religious and moral convictions.

Monseigneur Myriel fights injustice through charity, giving away his fortune to those who have nothing. He turns his palace over to the sick and gives his income away to charitable institutions. Although he is aware of social injustice—this is demonstrated in his sermon attacking the imposition of taxes on doors and windows in houses, which force poor people to live in dark, unhealthy, poorly ventilated housing—one would not view him as a critic of the social order (we have seen that his only explicit political standpoint is monarchist). Monseigneur Bienvenu's social philosophy seems quite simple: philanthropy and compassion are the arms that good men use to fight poverty.

This is exactly what the "good rich man" of the novel, Monsieur Madeleine, does, through his invention of a new system of black glass production that brings work and prosperity to Montreuil-sur-mer. "In less than three years the inventor of this process had grown rich, which is good, and had made everyone around him rich, which is better" (I, V, I, p. 167), observes the divine stenographer, making it clear that the book is not opposed to the rich, so long as they are like Monsieur Madeleine. The good rich man of the novel has set up a puritan, paternalistic system, vaguely reminiscent of the ideas proposed by the Scottish utopian Robert Owen. Men and women work in separate work-shops, and the owner is concerned with both their well-being and their probity. He has set up a sick bay for his workers, run by two Sisters of Charity. The men are asked to have "goodwill" and the women to have "pure morals," and both should be "upright." Monsieur Madeleine does not believe that his responsibility ends with the workers in his factory. The well-being of the whole area concerns him, and he builds hospitals, pays teachers out of his own pocket, and funds an old people's home. His philanthropy is so extreme that he secretly forces the locks of poor peo-ple's houses, steals into their rooms, and leaves a gold coin for them. He is firmly convinced that poverty is the mother of all vices, and that when this disappears, then "licentious behavior, prostitution, robbery, homicide, all the crimes, all the vices, will disappear" (I, VII, III, p. 241).

Almost all the critics of the novel, both conservative and progressive, have criticized the description of social prob-lems in *Les Misérables* for its lack of realism, exaggeration, omissions, falsehoods, and unreliability. From a Marxist perspective, Journet and Robert state that the novel is ". . . far from offering a representation of popular life. Long working hours and working conditions, employment insecurity, starvation wages, child labor, disease in working-class neighborhoods, a high death rate, all these questions concerned public opinion but, in the main, few people were concerned to analyze the causes of this deprivation. Victor Hugo situates his novel on another plane."[7] From a very different perspective, the skeptical Flaubert, who thought that the novel had been written "for the Catholic-socialist dregs, for all the philosophical-evangelist vermin," argued that the depiction of social life was excessively distorted: "Observation is a secondary quality in literature; but it is unacceptable to depict society in such a false way when one is a contemporary of Balzac and Dickens," he wrote to Madame de Genettes about *Les Misérables*.[8] In his "Considérations sur un chef-d'oeuvre, ou le danger du génie" (1838), Lamartine makes a savage attack on the book, which we will analyze in a later chapter. According to Lamartine, *Les Misérables* preaches "egalitarian socialism, the creation of unnatural systems," and, he adds severely, "You might note something surprising in this poem about enthusiastic workers: that no one works in the book, and that everyone is either out of prison or should be in prison, with the exception of the bishop and Marius, who embody religion and love."[9] The pious Narciso Gay states that the thesis of the novel is that "all the poor should be educated." This is because, he observes, the book believes that education will make them more upright and better people. How is it possible, therefore, that the aristocratic senator in the novel, a cultured man, is such a corrupt and pessimistic politician, such a repellent materialist? "Victor Hugo should admit to us, therefore, either that the education that he seeks for the poor is completely useless, or else that the rich who have received this education cannot in fact be the most immoral members of our society."[10]

Narciso Gay, like almost all the critics, states that it strains credulity to the limits to have Fantine lose her job for being a single mother. (This episode, along with Jean Valjean's five-year sentence for stealing a loaf of bread, were the two incidents universally accepted as being unbelievable.)

These and similar criticisms completely miss the mark. But Victor Hugo himself and the narrator made the task of such critics an easy one by declaring very openly that the book describes reality and expresses the truth. No, it describes a surreptitious unreality, fashioned out of reality. That is not to say that its view of society and social problems is a complete fabrication. Rather that, although one can pinpoint a great deal of accurate material on the injustices and inequalities in France at that time, the transformation that this material has been subject to in the novel is much more significant than its testimonial value, and that, fortunately for the novel, fictitious elements, as opposed to reality, are what prevail. The man who realized this, albeit for the wrong reasons, was Louis Veuillot, another reactionary critic of the time. In the *Revue du Monde Catholique* he argued that despite the book's being full of flagrant falsehoods and inadmissible exaggerations like the two mentioned above, these seemed "real" owing to "the immense power of Monsieur Victor Hugo's lungs."[11] He was on the right track, although he was wrong to consider as a moral failing something that is innate to fiction: the way that fiction transforms reality—exaggeration is one of its methods—and then presents its readers with a product that has been re-created through a technique and a style that make it appear "real" and "truthful." When a creator achieves this aim, the unreality smuggled in as life becomes part of reality, and the falsehoods become truths. For the "falsehoods" of fiction are accepted by readers when, by exaggerating, distorting, and disrupting human experience, they express a deep truth, which lies hidden behind the mask that writers don when they refashion lived experience in their work.

## A Society Rebuilt

This is what *Les Misérables* does with the social reality it portrays: it creates a fiction that is fictive to the highest degree, yet also sinks its roots in a specific history. It is not true, as Journet and Robert argue, that Hugo has turned his back on the most pressing problems of poverty and employment, or, as Lamartine argues, that in the novels no one works and almost all the characters are either common prisoners or else deserve to be in prison. But they are right to say that, through the craft of the fiction, the portrait of society that the novel paints is distorted in subtle and profound ways.

For example, in the fiction, work is a less important theme than the errors of the judicial system, the severity of penal legislation, the inhuman conditions in the prisons, and also prostitution, a theme that captivated the romantics. In the novel there are more idle people than workers, among whom we need to include thieves. There are many rentiers, like Monsieur Gillenormand, Jean Valjean himself, after he has made his fortune in Montreuil-sur-mer, the modest Monsieur Mabeuf; the bohemian students or the young rebels, the conspirators of the ABC, who live off, or struggle to make ends meet with, money from their families, or else live off their wits, or, like Marius, after he quarrels with his grandfather, take on part-time jobs, like Marius's translation work. The only person we see working from the beginning of the novel to the end is Javert, the perfect employee. But we also have an indication of the working conditions of the poor work through the character of Fantine. At first we see her working in Montreuil-sur-mer, happy and optimistic albeit somewhat unskilled, and later, when she is dismissed from the workshop as a result

of Madame Victurnien's prejudice, she works as a seamstress to earn a living and support Cosette. Her wages are
minimal. She has to sew for seventeen hours a day to earn
twelve centimes, and this goes down to nine centimes when
the prices in the textile market fall owing to prisoners com-
peting with the seamstresses. She sleeps scarcely five hours
a day and does not have even the most basic comforts:
"Fantine learned how to get through winter without a fire,
how to give up a tame bird that eats a tiny amount of food
every two days, how to turn a skirt into a blanket and a
blanket into a skirt, and how to do without a lamp by dining by the light from the window across the street" (I, V,
IX, p. 189). From this depiction we deduce that Fantine's
misfortune derives from her losing her job in the factory,
because the people who work there have a decent life and
are satisfied. The only negative aspect of the condition of
these invisible workers is the precariousness of their employment, because, like Fantine, they can be dismissed if
the bosses or supervisors detect any moral improprieties.
Workers who do not have "good bosses" are treated differ-
ently. For example, Champmathieu, who is about to be
sent to the galleys because he is taken for Jean Valjean,
gives us an idea of his life as a wheelwright when he makes
his semicoherent declaration to the court. He always works
out of doors, and, in winter, the foremen do not even allow
him to flap his arms to keep warm, because this is seen as
wasting time: "It's tough, handling metal when there's ice
on the street, you get old quickly . . . At forty, you're finished" (I, VII, X, p. 284). He earned barely thirty centimes
a day. Champmathieu's daughter, a washerwoman, spent
the day bent over a washtub, soaked to the waist come rain
or shine. "She died" (I, VII, X, p. 284).

This is a society, in short, in which there are more rentiers than workers, more idle people than those in employment, and more marginal people than well-integrated citizens. The most devoted and committed worker is a person who inspires in the narrator (and he tries to make the reader share his feeling) a deep moral repugnance: the policeman Javert. This is also a society in which there are more consumers than producers. Among these we must include the religious characters—the priests, the Sisters of Charity, the cloistered nuns—the thieves, the prisoners, the students and bohemians, the revolutionaries and the employees, the military and the marginal people. The heroes of the novel emerge from out of this mass of passive and ancillary beings. We have, by contrast, a more restricted view of the world of the producers: the workers, the artisans, the industrialists, and the professionals. There are very few characters, like Jean Valjean, who move from one category to the other.

There is an even clearer division in this society between rich and poor. But if we were to look for differences between the social classes based on their participation in the world of production, then we would be forcing the limits of this fictive society. In *Les Misérables*, strictly economic conflicts remain somewhat muted, while other divisions—based on names, titles, duties, rank, position—are given more prominence.

## The Victims: Confinement and Women

One important aspect of the novel, which gives it a modern feel—alongside its many antiquated social views—is the treatment of women. While there is no great opposition between workers and bosses, but rather an underlying harmony, the novel denounces in resounding terms the abuses suffered by women. They are referred to as slaves of the Western world: "We say that slavery has disappeared from European civilization, but that is not true. It still exists, but it affects only women and its name is prostitution" (I, V, XI, p. 196). In a passage later excised from part 3—"Marius"—in which the divine stenographer embarks on a long peroration about social problems, there is an even more explicit and extensive statement on the inferiority of women in society: ". . . when a woman is accepted by the social order, she is considered a minor; when the social order rejects her, she is a monster . . . One might almost say that women are outside the law."[12] Fantine illustrates this point: she is first treated as a "minor," then as "plagueridden." After she is abandoned by Félix Tholomyès, the young woman is on a downward path that ends in what the novel considers to be the most abject form of female decadence, prostitution, an institution on which society heaps all its opprobrium. The bourgeois character Bamatabois can play brutal jokes on Fantine, like putting a handful of snow down her back, between her bare shoulders, because a prostitute is not worthy of respect and is an object of derision. When she flings herself on her tormentor, it is she who is detained by Javert. He is disgusted that a prostitute can dare to insult and raise a hand to a gentleman who is a voter and who owns an elegant house. Javert models his feelings on the law, and it is likely, as he says, that if she were tried for this offense, she would be sentenced to at least "six months in prison" (I, V, XIII, p. 200).

Rather than a class struggle over vested interests, what causes conflict between people in the novel are prejudices, social, moral, and sexual prejudices. For that reason, the narrator is convinced that the remedy for crime and prostitution is schooling: "A thief, a public woman, are ill," he argues in another paragraph of the text excised from part 3: "open moral hospitals, that is to say, schools . . . What an admirable cure, to be cauterized by the light!"[13] Robbery and prostitution belong to the domain of history and can be cured: they are part of human responsibility; they are evils not caused by fate, that hand over which man has no power. However, there is an implicit contradiction in this idea. On the one hand, the novel argues that poverty and destitution are the root causes of theft and prostitution, and, on the other hand, it states that education will "cauterize" these evils. Can we deduce from this that the origins of poverty can be found in the lack of culture, the lack of education, among poor people? If that were the case, being cultured should be enough to ward off poverty, which is not true, because Monsieur Mabeuf, for example, in spite of all his reading and his knowledge, sinks gradually and irremediably into poverty.

## A Source of Social Injustice: The Law

We are given only a rather hazy idea in the novel as to how economic divisions, distribution of wealth, and working conditions cause misery and suffering. There is one aspect, however, that is made crystal clear: that a major cause of injustice and unhappiness is the law and the systems—the courts and the prisons—designed to apply the law and punish offenders. *Les Misérables* leaves the reader with the impression that judicial power and the prison system are civilization's Achilles' heel, that they bear the weight of responsibility for social injustice. In this world, men and women are born good, and society sets out to corrupt them with its inhuman and error-ridden institutions. That is why people feel terrified and threatened in this society, like Jean Valjean: "In the pale half-light in which he crawled, every time he turned his head and tried to look up, he saw, with terror mixed with rage, an endless structure rising above him, with horrible contours, a terrifying pile of things, laws, prejudices, men, and facts, whose shape he could not make out and whose mass appalled him, and which was none other than the huge pyramid that we call civilization" (I, II, VII, pp. 98–99). The law is a human institution and is opposed, rather than akin, to justice, which is divine. This distinction made by the narrator (I, VII, IX, pp. 277–283) is rigorously observed in the novel. The law makes many mistakes. The sentences are disproportionate to the offenses, like condemning a man to five years' imprisonment for having stolen a loaf of bread, or punishing a repeat offender with life imprisonment or the death penalty. The penalties, which are abstract, do not take into account the social context of the crime, like hunger and need that might be considered mitigating circumstances. The laws are similarly full of prejudices concerning sex and morality, like condemning a woman to six months' imprisonment for raising her hand against a gentleman, even in self-defense. Furthermore, the judicial system that applies the laws is riddled with errors, and the courtroom trial is a farcical spectacle. Champmathieu's trial is a ridiculous ceremony laced with black humor, in which the innocent man would have been condemned to life imprisonment or to death had it not been for the heroic sacrifice of Jean Valjean. In a supremely ridiculous moment, we see that Bamatabois, the man who attacked Fantine, is one of the judges. But if in fictional society laws are unjust and courts make mistakes or hand down excessive punishments, then the prison system is even worse. It acts with cruelty and impunity, and increases crime by training the criminal. Jean Valjean admits this when he confesses his identity to the courtroom in Arras to save Champmathieu: "Before going to prison, I was a poor peasant with very little intelligence, a kind of idiot. Prison changed me. I had been stupid, and I became evil. I'd been a log; now I became a torch" (I, VII, XI, p. 292).

Convicts are treated like wild beasts, without mercy, and become objects of public execration, as can be seen in the terrible spectacle that Jean Valjean and Cosette witness in the Barrière du Maine: the long line of prisoners, in chains and with shackles on their feet, who are being transferred to Toulon, lashed and insulted by their guards. If one of these men were to get out of that prison or survive the forced labor, he would not emerge from captivity as a reformed character, but, like Thénardier, who is captured by Javert after the ambush in the Gorbeau tenement, or like the villainous characters in the novel, rather as a more hardened and unscrupulous criminal than when he went in. And if, as happens to Jean Valjean, he sets out to be an honest citizen, his yellow passport will mean that all doors are closed to him, and that he will be hated and mistrusted by everyone. In these circumstances, only the intervention of a divine hand can guide this person away from wrongdoing that society maps out for him, and, like Jean Valjean, who is touched by grace through Bishop Myriel, keep him on the path of goodness.

## A Stupid and Cruel Monster

The most monstrous form of evil and error in the penal system is the death penalty, the guillotine, magnificently

roted—Victor was returning to France with his mother, having spent several months in Spain, where General Hugo was one of the right-hand men of Joseph Bonaparte—and who was advancing to his place of execution in a sinister procession, coupled with the image of the corpses of Spanish patriots executed and dismembered in Vitoria by the French, were to give him an early aversion to the death penalty. But there is another decisive event, a family tragedy: the execution in 1812 of his godfather, his mother's lover, General Lahorie, for conspiring against the emperor. This man, who had lived in hiding in the Hugo house in Les Feuillantines, and who doubtless had a good relationship with the children of Madame Hugo, because, to some extent, he replaced their absent father, was one day arrested by the police. A short time later, as a result of his absurd attempt at a coup, he was executed. Victor Hugo was ten years old, old enough to be affected by the brutality of this disappearance. It is likely that this experience—which, for obvious reasons, Adèle Hugo, in *Victor Hugo raconté par un témoin de sa vie*, refers to in an oblique manner—was at the root of the lifelong revulsion that the author of *Les Misérables* felt for capital punishment. In 1820, according once again to Adèle Hugo's account, he saw Louvel, the assassin of the duc du Berry, in the street, on his way to the scaffold, and "his hatred for the assassin gave way to compassion for the condemned man. He reflected on the matter and for the first time he faced the full implications of death penalty. He was surprised that society did to the guilty man, in cold blood and without any risk to itself, exactly the same thing as he was being punished for, and he had the idea to write a book against the guillotine."[15] In the summer of 1825, his friend Jules Lefèvre dragged him along to the Place de Grève to see a patricide,

Jean Martin, having his hand and head cut off. Victor Hugo was sickened by the festive behavior of the crowd gathered for the spectacle. On another occasion, he came across the tumbrel of a man about to be executed, a high-wayman called Laporte, while later he saw a couple of murderers, Malaguette and Ratta, on their way to the scaffold. He once crossed the square at the Hôtel de Ville and came face-to-face with the guillotine. The executioner was rehearsing the execution that was to be held that evening, oiling the joints of the machine while he was chatting amiably to passersby. According to Adèle Hugo, the day after this event, Victor Hugo began writing *Le Dernier Jour d'un condamné*, his first fictional denunciation of the death penalty, which he completed in three weeks and which was published in 1829 by the editor Gosselin.

At this time—between the ages of twenty-five and twenty-seven—there is evidence of a much broader concern that was not limited to prisoners sentenced to death, but included all prisoners and the penal system in general. His biographers tell us that on 22 October 1828, he went with David d'Angers to see how prisoners were chained and shackled and to learn prison slang.[16] Slang is an important ingredient in *Les Misérables*, because slang is the code that the Patron-Minette band use, and, more generally, it is the most frequently used way of differentiating the prison community from other groups and sectors in society. In any event, his second book on the theme of the death penalty, *Claude Gueux*, published in 1834, which was much stronger than his first, shows a deep concern with all these issues. His criticism includes the judicial system and the whole penal regime. For a long time it was argued that it was in 1828, while he was writing *Le Dernier Jour d'un condamné*, that Hugo heard from Canon Angelin the story of the ex-convict Pierre Maurin, who had received hospitality in the house of the bishop of Digne, an account that would form the basis of the characters Jean Valjean and Monseigneur Bienvenu. This account was originally cited by Armand de Pontmarin and was repeated by many critics, like Gustave Simon. (It is a story that is also used by Jacques Robichon, among others, in his fiction based on Les Misérables.)[17] But serious scholars, such as Jean Pommier, have rejected the story as an invention.[18] What is proven is that five years after publishing Claude Gueux, he was still interested in the fate of prisoners, because, at the end of the summer of 1839, after a trip with Juliette Drouet through the Rhine, Switzerland, and Provence, he visited the prison in Toulon to observe prison life. Seven years later, his curiosity about these matters remained alive, for on 10 September 1846, instead of attending a session at the Académie, he went to La Conciergerie and asked for the cells of this historic prison to be opened. According to Adèle Hugo, the previous year, in 1845, Victor Hugo had met someone in the Institut courtyard who would have given him firsthand information: an ex-prisoner, a former classmate at his school, the "Pension Cordier," little Joly. He had been orphaned as a young man, inherited a fortune, lost it all, got into debt, and had committed several crimes, for which he was "caught and sentenced to seven years in prison."[19] Victor Hugo gave him money, and the ex-convict often visited him at his house in the Place Royale.

The episode of the chain gang that Jean Valjean and Cosette meet at the Barrière du Maine is surely inspired by something that Victor Hugo saw, and which affected him profoundly, to judge by a speech that he made to the Assembly, arguing for an improvement in prison conditions, in which he refers in dramatic terms to this inhumane chain gang.[20] And throughout his career as a writer, during the time of the conservative monarchy as well as in the period of progressive liberalism, we can point to documents, attitudes, and initiatives that show that on these two issues—the death penalty and criticism of the prison system—Victor Hugo never wavered, and that, whenever he could, he expressed his views very clearly.[21] Here are a few examples of this coherent standpoint that he maintained throughout his political life, despite changing his mind on so many other issues. In 1832, for a reedition of *Le Dernier Jour d'un condamné*, he added a polemical preface against the death penalty. In 1834, he wrote to the king, asking, in vain, for the sentence on Claude Gueux to be commuted. In May 1839, however, he sent Louis Philippe a poem, exhorting him to spare Barbès, who had been condemned to death for leading a rebellion with Blanqui, and this time he was successful, as Barbès himself would acknowledge by thanking him for his intervention (thirty-three years later, in July 1862, when *Les Misérables* was published!). In 1848, he made a speech in the Constituent Assembly, asking for the abolition of the death penalty, and, the following year, he tried, unsuccessfully, to save another condemned man, by the name of Daix. He made a further statement against the death penalty in 1851, in the court that was trying his son Charles for having written an article against an execution in the newspaper *L'Événement*. In 1854, he wrote an open letter to the people of Guernsey, where a man was sentenced to be hanged, and on 2 December he wrote a splendid text asking for clemency for John Brown, a white American who had been sentenced to death for having led a revolt of blacks in Virginia against slavery. The open letter he sent to Lord Palmerston against the death penalty, dated Jersey, 11 February 1854, is another elegant text, both clear and forceful.[22]

This determination to denounce what he considered the inadmissible right of society to take the life of criminals, and to demand reforms to the judicial and penal systems, is clearly reflected in *Les Misérables*. All the scenes that deal with this issue have a particular force, and the "message" is always unequivocal and transparent. When it deals with these issues, despite the inevitable exaggerations that give artistic weight to certain scenes, the novel is also close to historic truth. But it is close to historic truth only if we isolate judicial and prison matters from the other social problems. Perhaps because the problem was one that Hugo was so passionate about, in the invented world this issue seems to be the basic and central problem of life itself, the root and foundation of all injustice. Work, income distribution, education, public health, political freedom, cultural production, and the like are all relegated to second place or disappear altogether in the overwhelming presence of the unhappiness caused by the evil called the Law. This unequal distribution of problems in the world of the fiction is what sets it apart from the "real" world. It is in this disproportionate reorganization, which suppresses some elements and maximizes and minimizes other elements, that we see clearly the "fiction," the "added element" in *Les Misérables*.

# CHAPTER VI

# *Civilized Barbarians*

While the novel is very clear and forthright in its attack on the death penalty, it is unclear on the issue of revolution, which is the subject of the tremendously powerful pages that constitute almost all the fifth part of the novel. The rebellion that *Les Misérables* describes is colorful, romantic, and poetic rather than historical, despite its being apparently based on a real event. In the "Epic of the Rue Saint-Denis"—written from beginning to end between 1860 and 1862—we find generosity, daring, fraternity, cruelty, violence, naïveté, stupidity, and, of course, misery and desperation. What we do not find is a clear view of what is at stake in the uprising. What do the leaders of the rebellion want? It is not even clear that they are antimonarchists seeking to overthrow the July Monarchy and establish a republic. When critics analyze this episode, they often make an extrapolation: they clarify the scene ideologically and historically, by filling in what the fiction leaves out with details from the real event. To this end, they make use of accounts by contemporary historians of the street rebellion that followed the funeral of General Lamarque.

By so doing, they betray the literary text, denying fiction its right to alter the reality that it purports to describe, and reducing what is essentially an invention to a mere historical document. Any attempt to compare fiction with a historical event merely serves to measure the distance, rather than the proximity, between them, and allows us to analyze the literary, ideological, and moral significance of the alterations that Victor Hugo has made to this reality.

## Long Live Death!

If, in real reality, the street uprising in Paris had a clear ideological content and a political goal—which is far from being true—in *Les Misérables*, there is none of this. These events in the novel have an epic and dramatic force, but it is very difficult to make sense of the ideas and intentions of the rebels of the Rue Saint-Denis from the information provided. The divine stenographer says that this was a "formidable and obscure" revolution (IV, XV, I, p. 1173). We must bear in mind the word "obscure."[1] The metaphorical speech made by Enjolras after he has executed old Cabuc to maintain revolutionary discipline is a moving, utopian description of a future society in which "the monsters will have given way to the angels and fatality will have given way to fraternity" (IV, XII, VIII, p. 1141). But the speech leaves us wondering what concrete steps must be taken to transform society into that paradise. Would it be through constitutional monarchy or a republic? What economic, social, political, and cultural measures would need to be taken? Who would rule and how would they rule? What laws would be abolished and what laws would be promulgated? There is not a hint of an answer to these questions in the idyllic, final vision of a future society that Enjolras evokes for his comrades. And the naive, sentimental speech by Combeferre is even less instructive. He is discouraging rather than impassioned, reminding the rebels to think of their wives and children and not to get themselves killed (V, I, IV, pp. 1207–1208). What exactly are the specific events, the injustices, the outrageous acts, the crimes, and the excesses committed by those in power that cause the uprising? What measures, laws, rules, and regulations do they want to abolish? What abuses do they wish to rectify? What guilty people do they seek to punish?

It is not by accident that none of this is explained in the vibrant, teeming pages of the novel. This is because in the fictional reality, these problems belong not to the historical domain, but to the domain of fate or divine predetermination. Men are agents through whom the unfathomable hand of God maps the course of history, which, as the narrator emphatically declares, is a steady march toward improvements in society and justice. "Progress is the lifestyle of man. The general life of humankind is called Progress; the collective march of humankind is called Progress" (V, I, XX, p. 1260). Just as the bishop of Digne was the incarnation of an idea—the idea of sanctity—so the rebels on the barricade of the Rue de La Chanvrerie personify the idea of history as a providential design that drives human life irresistibly—though time can be seen on occasion to be passing rapidly or else to be stagnating or going backward—toward justice and good fortune, this kingdom of social well-being that Enjolras glimpses on the horizon from atop the barricade. The rebels are the actors chosen to act out this idea of history on the world stage. For that reason, the "Epic of the Rue Saint-Denis" appears to be the most spectacular episode in a story in which, as we have seen, theatricality defines both characters and situations. The rebels seem not to be motivated to take up arms and take charge of their own destiny out of desperation, or a sense of exasperation, triggered by specific social and economic circumstances or political beliefs. Instead they seem to be eloquent interpreters of a script that they act out magnificently, but which also enslaves them. They are there, behind the stones, with their improvised arms and defenses, waiting for the troops to attack, waiting to sacrifice themselves and die, so that, through their death, the march of History can continue. Their attitude is grandiose, heroic, and sublime, but curiously passive, because it is obvious to everyone, in particular to the rebels, that the uprising does not have the slightest chance of success. They know and accept that they will be annihilated because this is the role that they must play in this drama of human progress, with its many tragic acts and its happy ending. That is why it does not seem strange to us when Enjolras's followers shout out the nihilistic slogan "Long Live Death!" (V, I, IV, p. 1206).

## Slow-Motion Progress

A similar theatricality turns the Battle of Waterloo in *Les Misérables* into a sublime performance in which the victors and the vanquished proudly perform the roles assigned them by a Supreme Being who is beginning to be irritated by the emperor of the French. "Was it possible for Napoleon to win this battle? We would answer, no. Why? Because of Wellington? Because of Blücher? No. Because of God" (II, I, IX, p. 344). God has decided beforehand the outcome of the battle. Now, if the end of the battle is al-

ready written before the fighting, the charges and the attacks, the deafening noise of the gunfire and the whistle of
the sabers, what is left for these combatants, who cannot
change the outcome of the chess game with its inflexibly
programmed moves, in which they are obedient pawns?
They are left with their performance, their formal skills,
the elegance and beauty with which they perform their
roles, embellishing them with romantic flourishes, like Ney,
who cries out that all the English artillery fire should be
directed at him, or sullying the role, like General Blücher
when he orders the execution of the prisoners. Thanks to
the marvelous way that reality is made unreal and history
is fictionalized in the chapter on Waterloo—like the epic
scenes in the Rue Saint-Denis that purport to describe the
street uprising of June 1832—the divine stenographer can
state quite justifiably that the true victor at Waterloo was
indeed Cambronne (I, I, XV, p. 356).

In fictional reality, revolutions are not an imperfect, cha-
otic, convulsive, ambiguous, collective movement that has
unforeseen consequences, but rather an ineluctable and impersonal phenomenon, beyond social limitations, like an
earthquake or a cyclone: "Revolutions come about not by
accident, but out of need. A revolution is a return from
falseness to reality. It exists because it has to exist" (V, I,
IV, p. 854). To understand what a revolution is, according
to the narrator of Les Misérables, one must change its
name—and, in this world of shifting identities, a change of
name indicates a change of role or function—and call it
Progress. And to understand what that word means, one
must change it to Tomorrow, or the future (II, I XVIII,
pp. 363–364). For "the stages of progress are marked by
revolutions"(V, I, XX, p. 1261). A destiny has been mapped
out since the beginnings of human existence that has im-

bued society with a dynamism which—despite having to face the severest of trials—drives it systematically toward higher forms of material, cultural, and moral life, as happens to Jean Valjean after his meeting with the bishop of Digne. Civilization always advances even when, at times, appearances seem to negate this fact and certain historical episodes appear to be a step backward.

The two historical events of the novel, the Battle of Waterloo and the popular insurrection of 1832, seem initially to be retrogressive. At first sight, Waterloo was the triumph of the counterrevolution, the triumph of the past over the present. But, according to the divine stenographer, "By ending the overthrow of European thrones by the sword, Waterloo merely caused the work of revolution to proceed in another form" (II, I, XVII, p. 364). As the empire had become despotic, he explains, the monarchies that defeated Napoleon had to set a different example, become liberal, accept the Constitution, and submit to the democratic reforms initiated by the French Revolution. In this way, the Revolution continued to make advances, in a vicarious manner, through the powers that were supposedly intent on stamping it out. The narrator is categorical: "Thanks to the Revolution, social conditions have changed" (IV, VII, III, p. 1020), and there is no reason for the jacquerie that followed, the anarchic social explosion of the wretched against the powerful, because from 1789 progress has become institutional, governed by the principle of "limiting poverty without limiting wealth" (IV, VII, IV, p. 1022). Popular uprisings start out as a mere riot, a stream that swells into a torrent, into an insurrection, which in turn sometimes runs into the ocean, which is the revolution (IV, X, II, p. 1079). Thanks to the French Revolution, there is universal suffrage, an admirable institution that cuts the ground from under the feet of violent revolt and, by giving insurrection the vote, disarms it (IV, X, II, p. 1079). Now, just because the people no longer have any reason to revolt, it does not mean that this will not occur. Because Progress can, on occasion, mark time, and poverty can drive the crowd, "which suffers and bleeds," to take up arms. But the crowd's "violence that runs counter to principles that are life-affirming, its attacks on the law, these are the popular coups d'état and must be suppressed. The man of probity stands firm, and for the love of the people, he must oppose them. But he understands them while he faces up to them and venerates them while he resists them!" (V, I, I, p. 1194). In one of his most beautiful and delirious sociopolitical perorations, the divine stenographer makes a distinction between "the barbarians of civilization" and the "civilized upholders of barbarism," and he states that, if he has to choose, he will choose barbarism. But, he adds, "there is, thankfully, another choice . . . neither despotism nor terrorism. What we desire is progress in slow motion" (IV, I, V, p. 871).

These ideas on history, human destiny, revolution, and human progress are a curious mixture of liberal, historicist providentialism with a dash of social democratic pragmatism. History is continuous progress, and its stages of development are certain grandiose upheavals called revolutions. The most important and, to some extent, the last of these stages is the revolution of 1789, which established the legal and institutional bases for Progress to be a "gradual ascent" without any sudden falls. However, since the elimination of poverty is a slow business, and there are checks and diversions in the march of progress, new revolutions will occur at times, which will have to be defeated so that history can continue on its ineluctable path, but which must also be understood, excused, admired, lamented, and extolled.

These ideas are not without originality. The divine stenographer argues them with stimulating vehemence and a battery of metaphors that we find seductive, but they remain, for all this, extraordinarily contradictory. This contradiction explains the shadows that surround the vibrant events of the epic struggle at the Rue Saint-Denis. The strategic aims in play, the demands and banners of the combatants, the political and social reasons for their rebellion are not clear because, quite simply, none of this is important to the supreme arbiter, this narrator who is convinced that the events of the barricade at La Chanvrerie are just one of the dramatic steps taken by History on its fateful journey toward human happiness. What the rebels think or want matters little or not at all: they are transient figures in a great design, a staging post on the long road to the luminous destiny of humanity described by Enjolras. The same can be said of the forces of order that attack the barricade and crush the rebels. Both are fleeting adversaries in a game whose rules have not been agreed and whose result will never be known.

## Victor Hugo and the Insurrection of 1832

But there is another reason why the "Epic of the Rue Saint-Denis" is ideologically "obscure." To explore this, we must now leave the fictional world and focus on what really happened and how the author came to know about those events, thirty years before transforming them into material for a novel. Victor Hugo had direct experience of the beginning of the insurrection of 5 June 1832. That day he was walking in the Jardin des Tuileries—this, according to the most erudite of his biographers,[2] was the way he had been working ever since his doctors had advised him to spend time in the open air among plants to help alleviate an eye infection—putting the final touches to the last scene of the first act of *Le Roi s'amuse*, when he saw that the public was being ushered out of the Jardin and the gates were being closed. He heard that an insurrection had begun following the burial of General Maximilien Lamarque. Lamarque, 1770–1832, was one of Napoleon's former generals and had been the military governor of Paris during the Hundred Days. He was exiled between 1815 and 1818, and then became a liberal deputy from 1828 until his death and one of the leaders of the republican party. Victor Hugo made his way "to the passage du Saumon," where the barricades were being erected, and suddenly found himself caught in cross fire. He was forced to take shelter behind shop pillars for half an hour. The anecdote is told by the narrator in *Les Misérables* (IV, X, IV, p. 1090) and repeated by Adèle Hugo in *Victor Hugo raconté par un témoin de sa vie*,[3] who adds that the day after the insurrection, Victor Hugo dined at the house of Émile Deschamps, where Jules de Rességuier told him about "the heroic defense of the Saint-Merry cloister." He based the epic descriptions that appear in *Les Misérables* on this account. While we have no reason to dispute these facts, we must not conclude, as a number of critics have done, that his description of the insurrection is faithful. In this episode as well, the "added element" is more important than what has been taken from real reality.

What was Victor Hugo's reaction to the street rebellion in 1832, where chance had placed him in the midst of the rebels and the forces of order? Solidarity? Sympathy for the rebels? We have no documentary proof. There are, however, more than enough clues to allow us to deduce that his reaction to the events was one of indifference, if not hostility. A note he wrote on the events of that day says, soberly, "uprising by the Lamarque procession. Madness drowned in blood . . ."[4] This is an objective, critical comment.

From July 1830, Louis-Philippe was in power in France and Charles X was in exile. Victor Hugo, who had been an "ultra" enthusiast of the Restoration, a regime that had given him annuities and gifts, but had also banned two of his plays, greeted the new regime with enthusiasm, with his poem "A la jeune France" (written on 10 July), which appeared in *Le Globe* on 19 August 1830. With the lifting of censorship, Hugo's previously banned works were performed, and in the preface to *Marion de Lorme*, in August 1831, Hugo spoke of the "admirable revolution of 1830," thanks to which theater "has gained its freedom amid a general freedom." His relations with the July Monarchy were even better than those he had had with the Restoration. To celebrate Louis-Philippe's first year on the throne, the government commissioned a hymn (set to music by Hérold), "L'Hymne aux morts de juillet," that would appear in *Les Chants du crépuscule*.

A state of siege was declared after the insurrection of June 1832. On 7 June, Saint-Beuve wrote to Victor Hugo, asking him to sign a declaration by writers in favor of "press independence," and that same evening Victor Hugo replied to him: "I will sign whatever you sign, despite the state of siege." But this declaration did not see the light of day. Victor Hugo replied to another angry letter from Saint-Beuve critical of the regime by agreeing with him, but also by making it clear that, in his opinion, the republican ideal should come about gradually, because France was not yet ready for it: "The Republic proclaimed by France in Europe will be the crown on our white hairs." The Republic was a distant ideal. In the present, the poet aligned himself with the regime of Louis-Philippe, which bestowed the highest honors on him, making him a nobleman, a peer of the realm. That morning on 5 June 1832, when he found himself in the midst of the firing in the Passage du Saumon, if Victor Hugo was close to anyone politically, it was to the July Monarchy and not to opposition sectors.

What were these sectors and which of them took up arms during the funeral of the old general? Historians of the period have had in the past divergent opinions on these issues, but today it seems clear that *all* the enemies of the July Monarchy—the opposition from the left, the republicans, and the Bonapartists, as well as from the right, the Legitimists and the Carlists—came to an agreement to organize a public uprising to coincide with Lamarque's funeral, and that they faced the army together.[5] So if we were asked what the rebels who got themselves killed on the barricades of Saint-Denis wanted, we would have to reply: different, incompatible things. The republicans wanted to abolish the monarchy and install a democratic, parliamentary regime based on universal suffrage. The Carlists and the Legitimists wanted to bring back the Restoration, that is, an absolute, traditional, ultramontane monarchy, and abolish the last vestiges of constitutionalism and liberalism. The Bonapartists wanted revenge against the traitors of Waterloo and those who had brought down the empire that they still hoped to restore. Can one think of a more heterogeneous mix? *Les Misérables* turns all of this into an astute abstraction: it dissolves these ideological differences into a sentimental and utopian haze that is so general in its

burglars, 40,000 public women who live off others, make
up a mass of 110–120,000 people who are difficult to manage. If Paris has 1,200,000 souls, and the number of criminals is 120,000, that makes one villain for every ten decent
people").[6] The admirable study by Louis Chevalier that
quotes these figures argues that in these years, never "were
the social and political antagonisms so strong, never were
there so many political upheavals, and never, despite economic expansion, and even at times of undeniable prosperity, was the poverty of the majority so acute."[7] The picture
painted by his work is terrifying: the poverty and unemployment of large sectors of the population led to crime,
suicide, infanticide, abandoned children, robbery, and assault, to such a degree that crime and the fear of crime
would be reflected in an entire, and very successful, literary
genre—the crime serial novel—which a masochistic public
read with a mixture of fear and delight.

But apart from the poverty-induced fear, terror, and
crime in the streets of Paris, there was another reason for
anxiety that immediately preceded the insurrection of 5
June 1832: the plague. The first victims were discovered
on 26 March, and by the 31st of the same month, some
300 cases had already been detected. The following day,
there were 565, with 100 deaths. The devastation caused
by the cholera epidemic would continue in the next days
and weeks, until it had claimed some 45,000 Parisian lives.
These ravages caused desperation and terror, especially in
the popular neighborhoods that lacked hygiene, where the
disease had originated, and also led to acts of violence. In
April and May, in the weeks preceding the burial of General Lamarque, in different parts of Paris, among the pesti-
lence and the deaths, there were riots, lynchings, and scenes
of collective madness. The rumor that criminal hands were

"poisoning the water" caused frenzied groups to attack army posts, while at the same time strangers and people outside the district who happened to stray into the neighborhood were sacrificed as scapegoats by an out-of-control mob that was searching for guilty parties, some way of dampening down the rage that they felt at this misfortune that struck indiscriminately. Social and political unrest was mixed in with these outbursts of savagery. There was a revolt by junkmen and a riot in Sainte-Pélagie prison, both of which were put down in bloody fashion.

This is the real context of the events of 5 June. Paris was up in arms for a number of reasons, ranging from the most general, the poverty of large sectors of society, to the most immediate, the ravages of the plague, which affected most particularly the poorest neighborhoods. Hunger, fury, fear, numerous antagonisms, an irrational need for revenge and sacrifice, all contributed to the explosion of this social powder keg. The spark that lit it was the disorder unleashed to coincide with the burial of the republican general.

Let us superimpose these two images, the image of historical Paris and the one that appears in the "Epic of the Rue Saint-Denis" in *Les Misérables*. What do we see? What is most important is not the similarities but the differences, the major changes that the artistic image has made to the historical view.[8]

For a start, this context of exasperation and chaos, of social violence and irrational outbursts, has disappeared. The plague has also disappeared—it is mentioned only obliquely at the beginning of the book entitled "5 June 1832," where the narrator states that it "had chilled men's spirits" three months before the insurrection—along with the heightened fear, fury, and hunger and the extraordinary confusion that led to the people's following the political agitators onto the barricades. How has this context been replaced in the "Epic of the Rue de Saint-Denis"? With a rhetorical smokescreen, one of those lengthy, tremendous speeches in which the divine stenographer, using Philosophy to eradicate History, holds forth, vaguely and elegantly, employing metaphor and eliding politics, on the differences between a riot and an insurrection and on the nature of revolutions, and makes subtle and lyrical comments on classical History—Greek and Roman—and on French history. It is true that his peroration finally gets up to the time when the events are taking place, but even then his analysis remains wordily innocuous, as he talks about the weakness of the July Monarchy and the hostility that it might have provoked, using images and metaphors that do not even remotely refer to the real political and social context of the Paris uprising of 5 June 1832.

It was not necessary for him to do so, for this was not his aim. *Les Misérables* is a fiction, not a history book. In fiction, historical events are pretexts that writers make use of to shape a different reality, and to speak of matters that obsess them, which have led them, sometimes consciously, sometimes unconsciously, to find a narrative form for these obsessions. The theme that Victor Hugo was writing about, when he rewrote—and transformed—the historical events of Waterloo and the insurrection of 5 June 1832, had little to do with social life, despite appearances, much more to do with the intimate life of the soul. And in its depiction of society, what the novel tries desperately to describe are the traces of a presence that, without ever being fully revealed, is the most important presence in the book, its essential context and its binding force: the mysterious hand of God.

CHAPTER VII

# *From Heaven Above*

When Victor Hugo began revising *Les Misérables*, after an interval of twelve years, he decided to add a "Philosophical Preface" to the novel. The rereading of the manuscript took him, according to some critics, from 26 April to 21 May 1860, although in his edition of the novel, Marius-François Guyard states that he finished on 12 May and that he wrote the preface between 26 July and 14 August.[1] In any event it is certain that he began to work on the preface immediately after he read through the manuscript. It took him all of June and July and the first weeks of August, an exceptionally long time for an author who was accustomed to writing a play in a few days and a novel in a few weeks. On 14 August he suddenly stopped work on the unfinished preface "to take up the main work once again." He never finished the preface, and, in its place, he published a few short lines as an epigraph, which stated that his novel could be of value while "the three great problems of this century" remained unresolved: the degradation of man in the proletariat, the subjection of woman through hunger, and the atrophy of the child by darkness.

By focusing on this short epigraph, many critics have concluded that the book's concerns are social, and that Victor Hugo was striving, in the novel, to combat the injustice, prejudice, and neglect suffered by workers and by women and children in France at that time. A reading of the enormous, unfinished "Préface Philosophique" reveals a more ambitious design: to demonstrate the existence of a transcendent life, of which life on earth is a mere transient part. The preface does not introduce a committed novel, rooted in the *here and now*, but rather seeks to give a theological and metaphysical justification for the existence of a first cause, and then to trace its appearance in the "infinite" history of mankind. It was not the opposition between justice and injustice that Hugo had in mind when he wrote his vast and fascinating "Préface," but rather the opposition between good and evil.

It consists of two parts: "God" and "The Soul." He completed just the first part; but he left quite an extensive draft of the ideas that he intended to develop in the second part.[2] In a brief preamble, Victor Hugo describes the nature of fiction and its relation to the real world: "This book has been composed from inside out. The idea engenders the characters, the characters produce the drama, and this is, in effect, the law of art. By having the ideal, that is God, as the generator instead of the idea, we can see that it fulfills the same function as nature. Destiny and in particular life, time and in particular this century, man and in particular the people, God and in particular the world, this is what I have tried to include in this book; it is a sort of essay on the infinite" (p. 311).

## The Enumeration of the Infinite

God, time, fate, and life are themes that are much broader than the historical and social context; these questions are, indeed, "infinite." The preface is an encyclopedic undertaking that is impossible to summarize. In it we find the creation of the stars, the dawn of life, the evolution of minerals, animals, and vegetables, the development of sciences and knowledge of nature, the emergence of philosophy, the appearance and the evolution of religions and the way they have given answers to the questions men and women have about their origins, the beginning of life, and their destiny. This strange text begins with a description of the earth, the seas, the wind, the stars, the comets, the organic and the inorganic, the infinitely large and the infinitely small. The scientific objectivity with which he talks, for example, about the sun—its distance away, its size, form, and composition—or the work of astronomers throughout history, or eclipses, is peppered by images that are like shafts of light shining through a darkness that is, at times, quite dense. However, although the detail, the exposition, and the information are at times vague or inaccurate, the author—and here we can talk of him rather than of the divine stenographer—never loses the overall direction of his account. Hugo does not forget that his text is a demonstration, not a description. For that reason, like staging posts on a journey, in the midst of this account of different phenomena, he suddenly includes a metaphysical parenthesis. For example, he interrupts a peroration on the Milky Way and the planetary system, in which "our" sun is scarcely an insignificant dot compared to the suns in other systems: "And the night is full of these lanterns of infinity. And what are the forms of life, of life in the world, of life in space? What moths will be burned in such places? Can you imagine what prodigious monsters they must be?" (p. 340). Like a watermark, philosophical, religious, and, at times, esoteric concerns appear in this summary of universal knowledge. The exposition takes on a poetic aura—"the normal state of the sky is darkness"—and is full of comments that give a religious tinge to the material universe, like the statement that the glacial cold and the darkness of space are a punishment imposed on creation. The philosopher thinks of all "the inexplicable forms of evil visible in life and sees rising up before him, like a backcloth, this terrifying reality, the world of darkness. This is suffering and, a sombre thought, it is a suffering that is the size of the universe" (p. 342).

The proof of the existence of God can be found in the limited resources that we have to solve the enigmas that are thrown up as science increases its scope. We know that each star has its own trajectory, but what is a "selenocentric" or "heliocentric" life? Why do comets move in ellipses, hyperbolas, and parabolas while the planets move in circles? To observe the world is to discover "the abyss, the abyss, the abyss." Faced with this combination of prodigies and enigmas, how can one be an atheist? "Faced with imminence, man is aware of his smallness and his short life span, and his night, and the unhappy limits of his sight. What is behind all this? 'Nothing,' you say. Nothing? What! I, an earthworm, am endowed with intelligence, while all this immensity is not? Forgive them, oh Abyss!" (p. 345).

Man is an "unspeakable miracle." The smallest and the largest things are mysteriously related. Even in mathematics, geometry and algebra, sooner or later something incomprehensible will arise. The "geometric point" is the meeting place of matter and abstraction, "the greatest

depths that the spirit can contemplate. Through this opening one can see God quite clearly" (p. 349). A long list
of Greek and Latin philosophers and thinkers who "have
prayed" illustrates the thesis that all philosophies end up
with "one finger placed on their mouths and one eye fixed
on the night" (p. 350). Religions are "the shadow the universe casts over human intelligence, and they all have a
common denominator. They all produce or use legends,
myths, rites, and similar forms, and almost all are the
source of certain prototypes that, like reclusive people, as-
cetics, and hermits, are repeated throughout time." This
proves "the tenacity of superstitions" but also that there is
not, and has never been, any thinking person on this earth
who has not been moved by the universe "to generate the
construction of a God." The only way to be a skeptic is to
deny the world and personality, and to affirm that everything is appearance. But this is a contradiction in terms.
Contemplation of the universe has led man to ask about
causes and the first cause, that is, God. Sacred terror gave
rise to religions that in turn gave rise to superstition. In
order to save men and women from superstition, philosophers tried to eradicate religions, and the result was mate-
rialism. What now remains of all this?

This is the end of the first part of the preface, which
attempted to justify rationally the existence of God. The
second part seeks to prove the existence of the soul, and
begins with the axiom "Life determines what is right."
Morally it is easier to smash a stone than to cut down a
tree, than to kill an animal, than to kill a man. But what is
the place of human beings in this order of things? Are they
tyrants? Are they executioners? Their powers are "omnipotent," as long as they have "progress" as their objective.
From this point of view, man "holds the power of life and

death over all inferior creatures. He is the terrible dictator of matter" (p. 365). But this power that he exercises over perishable matter is a sign that there is something in him that is neither matter nor perishable, something lasting, immortal, and that, thanks to this transcendent part of humanity—the soul—there is a "communication" between different aspects of creation: "Space is an ocean: the universes are islands. But there must be communication between them. This communication is made through souls."

From the second chapter, the text takes on a polemical tone to refute the atheism of liberals who believe in "the religion of humanity." The idea of democracy is inspired, he says, on the intuition of a secret and profound harmony between all things in the Universe. Man tries to reproduce in society the "solidarity" that links "everything with everything else." "Man shows solidarity with the planet, the planet with the sun, the sun with the stars, etc. . . ." Now, what allows us to perceive the intimate relationship among all entities is an "inner vision," a guide or lookout that man can rely on to take him beyond the limits of reason. Does that mean that, unlike reason, which can make mistakes, intuition is infallible? No, it can also make mistakes, but unlike rational knowledge, it "never loses sight of ideal reality . . . Its vision is the absolute." What would it mean to deny this moral dimension and just remain in the material world? It would mean identifying human beings with animals and things, denying freedom, and declaring the tyrant to be innocent. To admit the existence of the soul does not just allow us to understand freedom and make us responsible for our actions, but it also clarifies "the link between man and the Unknown."

If we limit ourselves to studying issues of freedom and responsibility in exclusively material terms, the conclusions reached could not be more pessimistic. Is legal responsibility not illusory in so many cases? Wrongdoers do not always pay for their crimes—"indigestion does not always punish the orgy"—and at times the innocent take on the burden of offenses that they have not committed. What remains if the moral responsibility that stems from the existence of the soul is suppressed? The most hesitant chapters of this second part, 6 and 7, attempt to distinguish between the "latent souls" and the "patent souls" and to interpret the night, a physical phenomenon, as a threatening temptation to moral health, since shadows stimulate doubts, anxieties, and lugubrious thoughts.

Men and women need certainties. Can they find them in science? Of course not, since scientific advances show the errors and gaps in society. They also show that the limits of reality are elastic and are constantly stretching, and for that reason it is futile to say, as some materialist democrats do, that they do not accept "supernaturalism." What is true is that, thanks to science, reality is expanding every day, to embrace what is distant (with the aid of the telescope) and what is very close (with the aid of the microscope). The "security" that human beings seek can be found only through faith, the belief in a moral law that would not exist if man were merely matter: "Democracy wants only to believe. For belief is power." On the other hand, God gives a religious and philosophical basis to the republican principle: "There is no king because there is a God; every monarchy is a misappropriation of privilege. Why? Because if one is not the author, then one has no right to authority." There then follows an argument against the monarchy and a defense of the idea that God desires "human democracy." The principle of a monarch by divine right is comprehensible among bees, because the queen is the biggest bee, she lives the longest, and, quite literally, she engenders her people. But among humans, do we find the same distinct superiority of one man over the rest? Men have been made equal: "My equal is not my master; my brother is not my father" (p. 384).

This line of argument becomes emotional and anecdotal in the lengthy chapter 11, in which Victor Hugo remembers his discussions in Brussels, in 1852, with the ex-priest Anatole Leray, an atheist and a materialist, who would years later sacrifice his life in Australia to save a drowning woman. He then moves the argument once more onto an intellectual plane by pointing out that religious fanaticism has caused terrible damage, and that superstition is atrocious. But would superstition be cured by the abolition of religion? Society can do away with churches, rites, and sacred texts. But would man be free as a result? When faced by a great misfortune, he would fall to his knees, like a mother who has just lost her son. Faced with the Unknown: "Mystery imprisons you once again. Or, better, it has never completely released you" (p. 390). It is true that the idea of a God who has created "evil" and who allows evil to continue is "incomprehensible." But is this a solid argument in favor of atheism? The incomprehensible—the infinite—surrounds us and yet still exists.

The following chapters develop the idea that "the absolute" is intrinsically just, and argue, mirroring the utopian ideas of Saint-Simon, that religious feeling exists outside established churches. It is legitimate to protest against the excesses and errors of the church, for this is "a deeper call to God." A thinker must protest not against religion but against the attitudes that falsify religion. Examining the human problem from any angle leads inevitably to the conclusion that something exists outside man, and that there is a link, which is both impalpable and unbreakable, that joins man to the Unknown. Prayer is an attempt at a dialogue with this shadow, and "anyone who has prayed knows that this shadow listens and replies" (p. 398). The last chapter—12—returns to the novel and summarizes the aim and meaning of *Les Misérables*: "Is this book heaven? No, it is earth. Is it the soul? No, it is life. Is it a prayer? No, it is suffering. Is it the grave? No, it is society.

"The earth can be seen only from heaven above. To achieve its aim, a study of poverty must implicitly offer two things: a warning to mankind and a prayer that rises to the heights . . . Reality can be painted effectively only in the light of the ideal.

"To paint misfortune, the whole of misfortune, that is, a dual misfortune—human misfortune that derives from fate and social misfortune that derives from man—is, doubtless, a useful undertaking, but for it to achieve its goal, which is progress, this undertaking implies also a dual act of faith: faith in the future of man on earth, that is, in his survival as man; and faith in the future of man beyond the earth, that is, in his survival as spirit.

"Works that echo with the laments of humankind must be acts of faith.

". . . I believe in God."

## Attempting the Impossible

Most critics of *Les Misérables* have paid little heed to this philosophical preface that seems at first sight to have nothing to do with the novel, a mere collage that the author himself ended up rejecting. One critic to have attempted an interpretation of the preface is Pierre Albouy.[3] In his opinion, the essay is a response to the political circumstances of the time. In the preface, Albouy argues, Hugo wants to *situate* God and the soul and also to prove that these beliefs, far from prejudicing democracy, are in fact indispensable to democracy. He is aiming the work primarily at democrats, republicans, and revolutionary atheists who had moved from anticlericalism to a denial of God. Hugo was surrounded by such people, like Auguste Vacquerie, Victor Schelicher, and Hamet de Kerles, and it was their ideas and attitudes that he had sought to refute in his book, by showing "God on earth, in humanity." Because Hugo was mainly interested in political problems, Albouy concludes, his plan for the novel was to "to have God become part of human society."

This analysis does not take into account that Victor Hugo had begun writing the novel many years earlier, and that his political and religious ideas had changed considerably over this time. Over this long period his ambitions for the novel had also changed. They had *increased*. Here we can draw an immediate parallel between the novel and the philosophical preface: both show excessive ambition; both attempt to achieve the impossible. Now that both texts are distant in time, readers today have no access to the issues being debated in that period. Instead all that survives is what strikes a chord with contemporary issues and sensibilities. This resonance is formal and literary rather than religious or political. Both the unfinished preface and the finished novel are impressive for their extraordinary determination to explore a topic to the limits, showing all its facets and ramifications. The preface seeks to demonstrate the existence of God by the most copious method imaginable: the description of the universe, beginning—as the Creator did, according to the Bible—with infinite space, the stars, the elements, matter, before finally reaching the privileged, superior being that is man, who combines the human and the divine. This endeavor is material and also spiritual, as it seeks to describe all the immaterial components of human history, the appearance and development of philosophical and religious ideas, of beliefs, superstitions, and dogmas, in order to trace the presence of God in this vast storehouse of existence. It is not surprising that, at a given moment, realizing the vertiginous nature of the enterprise, he should have abandoned this work.

Did Victor Hugo really put aside this philosophical preface forever on 14 August 1860? He continued it through a third party: the novel. I am not referring to the ideas and pages from the preface that he included in book 2 of the second part—"Parenthesis"—in which, with the pretext of criticizing the monarchy, he expounds his faith in God and the need for prayer, albeit outside organized religions, and rebuts atheism. I am referring to the more subtle, perhaps unconscious, way he transformed the intellectual concerns of the preface into the very substance of the fiction, which was already enormous and multifaceted, and which, over the following two years, would continue growing feverishly in all directions, through the amalgamation or juxtaposition of different material, until it reached overwhelming proportions and revealed, in its bulky plan, an intention that was as ambitious as it was fanciful: to write a *total* story.

## The Total Novel or the Deicidal Impulse

Let us return to this idea of totality, which is integral to any discussion of the novel. This temptation is present throughout *Les Misérables* and takes many different forms, beginning—as we have seen with the preface—with the sheer number of words in the story. The desire to include everything that can fill out the story and give it a life of its own, with no loose ends or gaps, has left its mark on both the structure and the explicit ideology of the novel. With regard to the organization of the narrative, this desire for totality has led to an emphasis on accumulating detail, on quantity, at the expense of the quality of the narrative structure. Spurred on magnificently by this deicidal impulse—imitating the Creator, creating a reality as numerous as the one he created, is a way of wishing to replace God, of wishing to be God—the divine stenographer adds themes and motifs, taken from the history of France, from the urban landscape of Paris, from religious issues, and from social and family gossip alongside, of course, inventions shaped out of the obsessions and passions of the author himself. But the narrator is hardly concerned with shaping these dissimilar elements into an organic whole. The lack of discrimination and measure with which the purely informative and descriptive material—the context—is presented makes *Les Misérables* appear out of proportion and somewhat monstrous, and this—especially in our day when literature tends to be intensive rather than extensive—intimidates the reader. The divine stenographer does not grade things for one very simple reason: in his world, as in the world of the Creator, nothing is spare; nothing is superfluous; the star and the pebble are the same; they are complementary parts of creation. At every stage in the novel we can see that if the deicide were not to impose some discipline, then the novel would never end; it would end up including all of creation, because each one of its episodes leads on to many others that, in turn, refer to others, in a chain with no beginning or end. The enormous

zac believed, "the private history of nations" but a more all-encompassing history than historians would write because historians record only important events, while for the novel, *everything* is important, the great events and the insignificant, trivial ones. This idea is marvelously expressed in the third chapter of part 1, "In the Year 1817," in which the narrator, in a dizzying enumeration, tries to recall all the events of that year, mixing major and minor events, episodes of historical importance and banal incidents. He ends with these instructive words: "Here is, all muddled together, what confusedly remains of the year 1817, now forgotten. History scorns nearly all these odds and ends and cannot do otherwise because it would be invaded by infinity. However, these details, which are wrongly called 'trifling'—there are no trifles in the human story, no trifling leaves on the tree—are useful. The face of the centuries is composed of the lineaments of the years" (I, III, I, p. 127). This is one of the narrator's most firmly held ideas, which he reaffirms at several points in the novel, almost always with the same words: "everything" is important; the details and the secondary aspects of the novel have the same human, moral, and social significance as the most striking incidents. "The facts that are to be related belong to a dramatic and living reality that historians sometimes neglect through lack of time and space. But it is here, we must insist, that life is to be found, the beating and tremor of human beings. Small details are, we have already said, the foliage of great events . . ." (IV, X, II, p. 1081). But where this idea of totality in the novel is most elegantly and perfectly expressed is in the description of the garden of the house in the Rue Plumet, where Jean Valjean and Cosette go into hiding when they leave the convent in the Rue Picpus. This whole chapter, the artistic high point of the novel, "Foliis ac frondibus" (Of leaves and branches), develops the idea that "rien n'est petit," that "tout travaille à tout" (IV, III, III, p. 904), and that there is a "flux and reflux" between the infinitely great and the infinitely small: "A cheese-mite is important; small things are large and large things are small; everything is in balance within the laws of necessity, a terrifying vision for the spirit. Between beings and objects there are prodigious relationships; within this inexhaustible whole, from the sun to the grub, there is no contempt; every thing needs every thing else" (IV, III, III, p. 904). There can be no finer description of the novel as a whole.

These views and convictions are those not of a man but of a God. They offer not a limited spatial and temporal perspective that, of necessity, narrows one's vision and forces one to discriminate and establish hierarchies between things and events, but rather the perspective of someone who has all of time in his favor and can embrace in his spherical gaze, which is at once both telescopic and microscopic, the entirety of space. It is only when one is freed from the human conditions of time and space that one can notice the deep, essential equivalence permeating the whole of existence. This is made even clearer if, with the help of the divine stenographer, we shift from the physical and historical plane to the moral plane . . .

In his curious criticism of the novel, which is both diatribe and praise, Lamartine predicted that it would do great harm to people, by making them feel "disgust at being people, at being men and women and not God." This sentence hits the mark in one sense. We readers do feel inferior to these superhumanly heroic or wicked characters, and even more inferior to the narrator, the God of the novel, who is convinced that "the eyes of the dramatist must be everywhere" (V, I, XVI, p. 1242), and is capable of making this wish come true because he has an infinitely wider perspective than any of us—and any of his creatures—when it comes to judging human actions: "One cannot be a good historian of people's outward, visible, resounding public life without being at the same time, to some degree, a historian of their hidden, private life; and one cannot be a good historian of this inner life without taking into account outward events when these are relevant" (IV, VII, I, p. 1007). What better way of saying that the novel is a description of the whole of humanity, and that a novelist must be omniscient, omnipotent, and ubiquitous.

From the superhuman heights where the narrator positions himself, the actions of men and women cannot be seen in the same way as from the reduced perspective of mortal beings, who are imprisoned by chronology and circumstance and are thus unable to understand all the developments and consequences of their actions. From his infinite perspective, by contrast, God can judge everything, and this allows him to be curiously unperturbed by temporal events, unlike man, who is an immediate victim or beneficiary of his actions. In the reality of the fiction, not all actions are good or bad; sometimes they are ambiguous or ambivalent and take on different meanings from different points of view. On the battlefield of Waterloo, Thénardier saves Colonel Pontmercy from the mound of bodies that are covering him, but he does so with the intention of robbing him. The narrator-God, who reads thoughts, knows that the innkeeper from Montfermeil committed this act with wicked intentions and condemns him. But is it justified that Marius's father should spend the rest of his life feeling eternal gratitude for the man who saved his life? Whatever the reasons Thénardier had for acting in this way, for Marius's father it is enough to know that the man rescued him from among the bodies of his troop and that he is alive thanks to him. Objectively, Thénardier did a good deed, although subjectively it was bad. The narrator-God is conscious of this contradiction, but he does not draw from it the alarming conclusion that there is a moral relativism to human life, and that there are contradictory values. He emphasizes the contradiction only to show that man's knowledge of other men is precarious and prone to error, and that his moral judgments are thus insufficient and frequently wrong. For God, who is spirit, the spiritual is the dominant reality, and it is in the intimate, deep, and imperceptible life of the human soul that what really counts takes place, while what is manifest in the exterior, visible, objective, social world is secondary. This idea is clearly expressed in the "affaire Champmathieu." In that night of doubts and moral torment that precedes his decision to hand himself over to justice to prevent an innocent man from being condemned, Jean Valjean ponders this problem. Should he give himself up even though this will do enormous harm to Montreuil-sur-mer, which lives from his industry and benefits enormously from the work he has created as well as from his philanthropy. Should one ruin a town to save an innocent? This is what happens when Jean Valjean goes to prison to do his duty to his conscience and to God. His factory goes bankrupt, and poverty and unemployment grip what had once been a thriving community. So serving God can mean harming society. The narrator-God knows this very well, since he says it, but the problem of "contradictory values" does not exist for him, because, from his perspective, there is no lesser evil. There is good or bad; there are good or bad actions. Ambiguity, contradiction, and ambivalence are manifestations of a limited human condition: they do not exist in divine wisdom. From the standpoint of this wisdom, Jean Valjean acts "well" when he gives himself up, and if he has had to overcome the scruples that he feels at causing harm to the community of Montreuil-sur-mer by his actions, this makes his character more honorable as well as more dramatic. In the all-embracing vision of God, in physical reality, the infinitely small and the infinitely large are equivalent. The same is true in spiritual reality: the only accepted division is what separates good and evil, good intentions from evil intentions. Within this completely polarized view of human conduct, all behavior is equal in the timeless and ahistoricist gaze of God. The idea of relative values, conditioned by social, family, or individual circumstances, is irritating to God. In his divine eyes, all this simply reveals the inadequacies and defects of human beings. The action Enjolras takes on the barricade, for example, when he kills a man in cold blood to save the lives of many others is, for divine morality, somewhat barbarous and unacceptable because, from this perspective, what counts is not the act itself but its hidden motivation, its abstract, timeless source, removed from any context, and from this perspective it is a matter of indifference that one person dies, or a hundred or a thousand: they are merely a colorful detail in the monotonous moral landscape of absolute values.

This belief in God, emphatically defended in the philosophical preface, is closely linked to the deicidal (the divine) features of the eponymous, Olympic, thunderous, and (above all) "totalizing" and all-embracing narrator of *Les Misérables*. Without the foundations of a belief in such a being, it would be impossible for a writer of the mid-nineteenth century to create a narrator with such prodigious attributes as we have seen in the divine stenographer.

The process of making the narrator of a novel invisible or disguised begins, precisely, with the weakening of faith, with the degrading of a certain image of God, or of God himself. It is not coincidental that the first novelist to sound the death knell for the all-powerful, omniscient, omnipotent, ubiquitous, and visible narrator-God was Flaubert, a religious skeptic. The death of the narrator-God is a formal consequence, in fiction, of the death of God in the hearts of men and women.

In *Les Misérables*, we are apparently still far from this process (although it was already happening with the publication of *Madame Bovary*), and God thunders and rules, vast and formidable, beneath the skin of the divine stenographer. The epic that he narrates does not really take place in the exterior and objective world of human acts. The world so prolifically described and explored in the novel is a mere set for the profound drama that the narrator-God wants to recount: the redemption of man, his irresistible and tragic march toward goodness, the redemption of Satan by the Divine Being. Even though the verses of "La fin de Satan," Hugo's ambitious and unfinished theological prophecy that at the end of time, infinite divine compassion would end up establishing a reign of absolute goodness—God would forgive Satan and he would be redeemed, like Jean Valjean—was still to be written, we find that in *Les Misérables*, a novel that the author always considered a religious book, there appear already the glimmerings of the audacious proposition that sin, evil, suffering, and misery would be eclipsed one day with the return to divine glory, through God's forgiveness, of Lucifer, the fallen angel.

# CHAPTER VIII

# The Temptation of the Impossible

Contrary to widespread belief, when *Les Misérables* was first published, not all the commentaries and articles on the novel were enthusiastic. There were many adverse criticisms, some of which, like the article by Barbey D'Aurevilly, were very hostile indeed. The most interesting of these critical commentaries, because of the issues that it touches upon and because, using Victor Hugo's novel as a starting point, it develops a number of bold ideas about fiction in general, is the long study by Alphonse de Lamartine. In his commentary, perhaps without intending to do so, Lamartine deals head-on with the function of fiction in history.[1]

At the beginning of his essay, the reservations that he has about the novel come from a conservative who sees *Les Misérables* as a text that might encourage disorder and social unrest, and a supporter of literary realism who is irritated by the exaggerations and inaccuracies of the book when compared to the reality that it purports to re-create. According to him, *Les Misérables* "makes an imaginary man the antagonist and victim of society." "Man against society, this is the real title of the novel, a disastrous work because while it presents individual man as a perfect being, it regards human society, constituted by men and for men, as a synthesis of all human iniquities" (p. 306).

The novel, for Lamartine, is a utopia following in the tradition of Plato's *Republic*, Rousseau's *Social Contract*, and all socialist traditions from Saint-Simon to Fourier, Proudhon and even the Mormons!

As he recollects his own involvement in the Revolution of 1848,[2] Lamartine recalls that at this time Victor Hugo had published a "conservative" manifesto that he had thought very sensible. Lamartine attacks "demagogues and utopians" and argues that *Les Misérables* offers "an excessive, radical, and sometimes unjust critique of society, which might lead human beings to hate what saves them, which is social order, and to become delirious about what will cause their downfall: the antisocial dream of the *undefined ideal*." This ideological *lack of definition* seems to him to be the most negative aspect of the novel's utopianism.

The title, he assures us, is false, because the characters are not *misérables* but rather *guilty* and *lazy*. In the novel, almost no one is innocent, since nobody works. It depicts a society made up of thieves, dissolute characters, layabouts, women of the night, and street urchins. Not even when they act do the characters understand what motivates their behavior. For example, if one were to ask Marius why he is on the barricade, he would not know what to reply: "par ennui," perhaps (out of boredom), but not "out of conviction."

The novel is an "epic of the rabble," "a masterpiece of impossibility" (p. 364). From this point on, Lamartine's observations, while still remaining political and literary, extend into the realms of religion and philosophy. Broadening his argument beyond Hugo's novel, Lamartine goes to the heart of the relationship between fiction and history and the way that fiction influences life and society.

*Les Misérables* will do a great deal of harm to the people, "making them feel upset that they are men and not God." Lamartine has an imaginary conversation with "a prisoner condemned to death," who has been forced to read the novel. Both agree that Jean Valjean is a monster for having robbed the good bishop and the child Petit-Gervais, and both accuse the book of being exaggerated and unrealistic, although they argue that Hugo's "talent" for realism makes the reader accept it as real.

Although the character of Monseigneur Bienvenu seems "exemplary" to him, Lamartine is upset at the conversation between him and G the Conventionist, which he considers to be "a deification of terrorism." And he vigorously refutes the "abstract mathematics" that justifies the crimes committed by the Jacobin Terror in '93 on the basis of the crimes that the poor were subject to in the past. Are classes always the same throughout time? Don't they rotate and change? Such an argument means "praising the people for their lowest instincts," which is like telling them, "You are right to be angry and to kill, for then writers like Victor Hugo and Joseph de Maistre, the first a democrat, the latter an autocrat, will come and justify your killing with their theories."

He accuses Monseigneur Bienvenu of ignorance for criticizing taxes "that are the levies that the rich pay to the poor to make them more equal." If the taxes were abolished, the victims would be the proletariat who receive funding from the state. Similarly, if "luxury," that is, consumption, were abolished, then production would come to a halt and the victims would be the producers, in the country or in the city.

It is good, Lamartine argues, that Victor Hugo is drawn to the problem of human suffering, like so may writers since Job, but why accuse society of being responsible for all misery? Has society created life? Has it invented death? Is it society, finally, that has produced inequality, which is both inexplicable and an organic part of nature and the human condition? No, it is not society, but God. Feel sorry for society, give it advice, that's fine. But don't put it in the dock, for that is to behave in an unthinking and barbarous manner (pp. 429–430). "If we sow ideal and impossible thoughts in the masses, we reap the sacred fury of their disillusionment" (p. 431).

The chapter in *Les Misérables* entitled "In the Year 1817" seems treasonable to Lamartine. Why these sarcastic remarks and these jokes at the misfortunes of "the princes who protected the childhood" of Victor Hugo himself. And Lamartine reminds the author of the novel that Chateaubriand once called him the "sublime child."

The episode with the bohemian students and their young lovers—Fantine among them—is, for Lamartine, a total failure. He likes the scene with the Thénardier girls on the swing; but, in contrast, he finds the misfortunes of Cosette's mother—in particular when she sells her teeth and her hair—to be melodramatic and false. The novel "becomes unrealistic as it becomes appalling."

He gives Monsieur Madeleine's being sentenced to the galleys as an example of this lack of verisimilitude: "The world is not like that." He is one of the critics who are indignant that Victor Hugo spelled out the *merde* uttered by Cambronne, and, above all, that he calls this word "the most beautiful" in the French language: "The narrator loses his wits to such an extent that he confuses the ignoble with the sublime" (p. 66). "This word adulates the base instincts of an enraged crowd that cannot articulate its grievances and, instead, throws excrement in the face of destiny. It is an example of grammatical demagogy that, in an attempt to make everything equal, deprives the soldier and the people of an immortal relic, replacing it instead with . . . something disgusting" (pp. 77–78).

For Lamartine, the purely fictive elements in the novel are its weakest part: "All the fictional parts that are based on events arbitrarily invented for the purpose of the drama are the weak points of the novel. Every time the author needs a character, he summons it up from nowhere, as in fairy stories or in Voltaire's stories, and the character obeys, against all plausibility, the call of the writer" (p. 84).

He accuses Victor Hugo of wordiness, of making an "exhibition of knowledge about trivia." He sees that Marius is a self-portrait of the author as a young man, and he considers the description of the courtship between Cosette and Marius to be "the most delectable love scene" that Victor Hugo has ever written. By contrast, he finds it ridiculous that the events in the Rue Saint-Denis are called "Epic," since they are merely "a heroic fantasy of idle students . . . with no definite idea, no practical means, and no stated and defensible objective."

On the "epic" of Saint-Denis, he adds that the rebels are fighting for something that no one can identify, an enigma, "that is not the legitimate monarchy, or the secondhand royalty of 1830, or the Republic proper, or any definite form of government, but something, I don't know what exactly, that is sometimes called democracy, and sometimes called the ideal, and which is, in fact, the red flag" (p. 149).

In short, for Lamartine, *Les Misérables* is a dramatic, exaggerated, horrifying story, full of social and political "chimeras," a novel that would not survive were it not for

Hugo's enormous verbal talent and lyrical strength, which can bestow a semblance of reality on these "unrealities."

From these premises, Lamartine concludes that the novel is "dangerous" for the people because of its "excess of idealism": "The book is dangerous, because the supreme threat to harmonious society is excess, which seduces the ideal and perverts it. It gives unintelligent men a passion for the impossible: the most terrible and the most homicidal of passions that one can instill in the masses is the passion for the impossible. Because everything is impossible in the aspirations of *Les Misérables*, and the main impossibility is that all our suffering will disappear" (p. 186). "If you deceive a man, you will drive him mad; and when, from the sacred madness of your ideal, you let him fall again into the arid nakedness of his misfortunes, you will turn him into a furious madman" (p. 187).

His final words are a frontal attack on the narrator's conviction that "limitless progress" is possible. Such optimism ignores "the force of things," that is, the limitations inherent in the human condition.

What started out as literary criticism ends as a sociopolitical condemnation of a whole genre that Lamartine—using much the same arguments as did the Spanish Inquisition in the sixteenth century, which banned the publication of novels in the American colonies—accuses of unsettling "the masses." It makes them have aspirations and desires that are out of the reach of ordinary mortals, thus turning them into a source of rebellion and social unrest. In his lengthy essay, Lamartine thinks that he is aiming his barbs at a precise target: at that prodigious fictional construct, *Les Misérables*, which, owing to the remarkable talent of its author, can make the readers believe that a human being is capable of the extraordinary moral grandeur and self-sacrifice of a Jean Valjean or the angelic goodness of a Monseigneur Bienvenu, both of which are romantic "unrealities." But, in fact, his argument holds good for all successful fiction, even fiction that does not have the scope and sweep of *Les Misérables*, because, through its persuasive power, fiction transports readers into a world that is more coherent, more beautiful, more perfect, or simply less boring and miserable than the one they inhabit. According to Lamartine, once the readers, who have been bewitched by the novel, finish the work and find the spell broken, and that the life they lead cannot measure up to the life they dream, they will become "unhinged" and turn into furious rebels, into enemies of the established order.

Lamartine's reproach to Victor Hugo reminded me of an observation by the historian Eric Hobsbawm, who argued that what the German princes most feared in their subjects was "enthusiasm," because this, in their opinion, was the seedbed for rebellion, a source of disorder.[3] Lamartine and the German princes were right, of course. If the object is to keep society within strict limits, subject to an immutable order like stars or a rail timetable, the "enthusiasm" and the temporary enchantment that a successful fiction produces can be seen as a powerful enemy, an element of unpredictability that can disorganize life, sowing doubt and discord, and encouraging a spirit of criticism, a solvent that can open up multiple fissures in the structure of society.

Lamartine was right to consider that "the passion for the impossible" was a dangerous disease that might infect the masses, because he had paid for this passion in his own life. Throughout his life, he and Victor Hugo had maintained friendly relations and mutual respect. For example, Lamartine was one of Hugo's sponsors every time the author of

*Les Misérables* applied for membership of the Académie Française. He was successful on his fifth attempt. Their correspondence reveals a cordial relationship and an admiration for each other's work. They had a number of things in common: talent, a facility for writing, a love of politics and social esteem, and both achieved in their lifetime most of what they had set out to achieve. But Lamartine reached the pinnacle of political power, albeit briefly, something that Hugo never managed. Lamartine was one of France's civic heroes in the downfall of Louis Philippe, in February 1848, and became head of the provisional government of the newly proclaimed Republic. He was also the deputy to receive the most votes in the April elections for the first National Assembly. As one of the five members of the Executive, he had to face the great uprising at the end of June 1848 by a people fired with revolutionary enthusiasm, who felt that their rulers were not living up to their expectations. This event ruined his political career. His time in power was fleeting, from February to June 1848. To combat these "masses" that were filling Paris with barricades, the government that he belonged to gave special powers to the war minister, General Cavaignac, who drowned the uprising in blood, with widespread executions and ferocious repression. It seems that from that moment, Lamartine, whose political star would never again be in the ascendancy after that failure, had a visceral distrust of anything—like fiction, in his opinion—that could offer the masses the temptation "of the impossible."

It is difficult to agree with many of Lamartine's comments on *Les Misérables* because it is clear that they are often unjust and exaggerated. But one should also recognize that his study of the novel does contain an accurate intuition as to the nature of literary fiction and its impact on readers and on society in general. He concentrates his criticism on *Les Misérables* because he perceives in this work a danger that he does not see in other novels, for the simple reason that they lack the extraordinary ambition with which Victor Hugo's work has been written, this novel that, by its very scale, competes with reality on an equal plane, offering a "total" fiction in place of life.

It is the case that, albeit to a lesser extent, all fictions make their readers live "the impossible," taking them out of themselves, breaking down barriers, and making them share, by identifying with the characters of the illusion, a life that is richer, more intense, or more abject and violent, or simply different from the one that they are confined to by the high-security prison that is real life. Fictions exist because of this fact. Because we have only one life, and our desires and fantasies demand a thousand lives. Because the abyss between what we are and what we would like to be has to be bridged somehow. *That was why fictions were born*: so that, through living this vicarious, transient, precarious, but also passionate and fascinating life that fiction transports us to, we can incorporate the impossible into the possible and our existence can be both reality and unreality, history and fable, concrete life and marvelous adventure.

It is enough for a fiction to be successful and to make its readers share the illusion for this miracle to occur. The fact that Lamartine singled out *Les Misérables* was a way of recognizing the wider aims of the novel, a creation that, with its irresistible power of persuasion, could, by making its readers restless, become an unsettling force in society, like the force that in June 1848 stripped the streets of Paris of their stones to build barricades and ended his political leadership.

Alphonse de Lamartine's fears will seem laughable to many. Who today thinks that a great novel can subvert the social order? In the open society of today, there is an idea that literature in general, and the novel in particular, is a (perhaps superior) form of entertainment and amusement, an activity that is enriching and stimulating, but which, above all else, is a way for readers to have a good time, to compensate for their boring routine and petty everyday worries. Since there is no way of proving in real terms that the most important works of literature, from Shakespeare's tragedies to the novels of Faulkner, via *Don Quixote* and *War and Peace*, have caused even the slightest ripple of political or social unrest, this idea of literature as an entertaining and *inoffensive* activity has become common currency in today's open societies.

Is this the same in closed societies of whatever form, be they religious or political? It was not just the Spanish inquisitors who had an instinctive distrust of novels, seeing them as destabilizing and undermining faith. All the dictatorships that the world has seen have imposed systems of censorship on literary creation, convinced that the free invention and circulation of fictions could jeopardize the established order and erode discipline, that is to say, social conformity. In this, fascists, communists, religious fundamentalists, and third world military dictatorships are identical: they are all convinced that fiction is not, as naive democracies might believe, a mere diversion, but an intellectual and ideological time bomb that can explode in the mind and imagination of its readers, turning them into rebellious dissidents. The Catholic Church agreed with Lamartine and put Victor Hugo's novels on the Index of banned books in 1864 as being dangerous to the health of believers.

Dictatorships exaggerate this susceptibility, which is not surprising because a typical characteristic of all authoritarian power is paranoia, a sense of living in fear and permanent suspicion of everything and everyone, seeing enemies on all sides and inventing enemies if they do not exist in order to justify the censorship and repression that give them a feeling of security.

They exaggerate, but they are not wrong. In societies where all the means by which citizens can express their opinions and desires and register their criticisms—the press, political parties, elections—are closed down, then literature automatically takes on a significance that extends beyond the literary and becomes political. Readers read these texts between the lines and see (or think they see) what they cannot find in the media that have become organs of propaganda, where information is concealed, ideas are banned, and criticism is shackled. Whether or not this is the authors' intention, in such circumstances literature takes on a subversive role, hounding and questioning the social order.

Why subversive? Because the beautiful and ideal worlds—the "impossible" worlds, Lamartine would argue—that fictions create for their readers show them, by contrast, the imperfections of the world they live in and confront them with this obvious fact: that "real" life is petty and miserable in comparison with the splendid realities that successful fictions construct, in which the beauty of the words, the elegance of the construction, and the effectiveness of the techniques are such that even the most ugly, low, and abject things shine forth as artistic triumphs.

It is not exactly "enthusiasm" but rather unease that good fictions leave in the minds of their readers when they contrast these images with the real world: the feeling that the world is badly made, that life as lived is very much poorer than what can be dreamed and invented. Nobody is trying to argue that this unease inevitably and automatically leads to an "enthusiasm" for action, a desire to act in some way to change society, to shake it free of its inertia and make it more like the model worlds of fiction. For it does not matter if none of this occurs. This unease is in itself subversive in regimes that attempt to control the whole individual (their thoughts, actions, and dreams), regimes which consider that, because of fiction, the thoughts and fantasies of their citizens are out of their control, even though outwardly they still appear docile. Thinking and dreaming openly is the way that slaves begin to become restless and discover their freedom. Without meaning to— he was looking rather to discredit Victor Hugo's novel— Lamartine paid a great tribute to *Les Misérables*. Because there is no better way of praising the creation of a writer than to say that the force of its pages is so strong that it can brush aside the sober reason of its readers, and convince us that its chimerical adventures, its larger-than-life characters, and its gruesomeness and wild imaginings are indeed true human reality, a reality that is both possible and achievable. It can convince us that this reality has been stolen from us by bad governments and the evil arts of evil men, who hold power on earth and exploit and dominate society, but that reading gives us access to this lost reality and spurs us on to recover and reinstate it through our actions.

There is no way of demonstrating that *Les Misérables* has moved humanity even a few inches along the road to the kingdom of justice, freedom, and peace that, according to Hugo's utopian vision, is the path of humanity. But there is no doubt, either, that, in the history of literature, *Les Misérables* is one of the works that has been most influential in making so many men and women of all languages and cultures desire a more just, rational, and beautiful world than the one they live in. The most minimal conclusion that we can draw is that if human history is advancing, and the word "progress" has a meaning, and that civilization is not a mere rhetorical fabrication but a reality that is making barbarism retreat, then something of the impetus that has made all this possible must have come—and must still come—from the nostalgia and enthusiasm that we readers feel for the actions of Jean Valjean and Monseigneur Bienvenu, Fantine and Cosette, Marius and Javert, and all who join them on their journey in search of the impossible.

Lima
3 February 2004

# Notes

INTRODUCTION: *Victor Hugo, the Ocean*

1. "E.g., This morning. Everything. Everything." "Mlle Rosiers. Legs." "Marianne. The first time." "Ferman Bay. Everything taken. 1fr 25." "Saw a lot. Took everything. Osculum."

CHAPTER I: *The Divine Stenographer*

1. All the quotations are taken from the La Pléiade Edition (Paris: Gallimard, 1951).
2. Henri Guillemin, *Pierres* (Geneva, 1951), p. 61.
3. Narciso Gay, *Los Miserables de Victor Hugo ante la luz del buen sentido y la sana filosofía social* (Madrid: Librería Española-Barcelona, Librería del Plus Ultra, 1863), p. 257.

CHAPTER II: *The Dark Vein of Destiny*

1. Barbey D'Aurevilly, *Les Misérables de M. V. Hugo* (Paris, 1862), p. 46. "The ants' nest that everyone must fall into . . . like insects into the ants' nest."
2. Letter quoted by Raymond Escholier in *Un Amant de génie: Victor Hugo* (Paris: Arthème Fayard, 1953), p. 150.
3. *Les Misérables*, Edition de L'Imprimerie Nationale (Paris: Paul Ollendorf, 1908–1909), vol. 1, *Fantine*, p. 406.
4. Marx reproached Victor Hugo for attributing the development of history to certain exceptional individuals. In the prologue to the second edition of *The Eighteenth Brumaire of Louis Bonaparte* (1869), he criticizes the author of *Napoléon le Petit* for interpreting the coup of 2 December 1851 as "a bolt from the blue." And, he added, "He does not notice that

he makes this individual great instead of little by ascribing to him a personal power of initiative such as would be without parallel in world history." Karl Marx, *The Eighteenth Brumaire of Louis Bonaparte* (London: Lawrence and Wishart, 1954), p. 6.

CHAPTER III: *Touchy Monsters*

1. André Maurois, *Olympio ou la vie de Victor Hugo* (Paris: Hachette, 1954), p. 145.

2. This episode, which was added in the 1860–1861 version, caused a scandal and was the passage that was most attacked by ultramontane critics when the novel was published.

3. Quoted by Bernard Leuilliot, "Commencement d'un livre," in *Lire Les Misérables* (Paris: José Corti, 1985), p. 61.

4. Mme. Richard Lesclide, *Victor Hugo, intime* (Paris: Félix Juven, 1902), p. 197.

5. Henri Guillemin, *Hugo et la sexualité* (Paris: Gallimard, 1954), p. 96.

6. Pierre Albouy, *La Création mythologique chez Victor Hugo* (Paris: José Corti, 1963), pp. 200–201.

CHAPTER IV: *The Great Theater of the World*

1. Guy Rosa, "Réalisme et irréalisme des Misérables," in *Lire Les Misérables* (Paris: José Corti, 1985), p. 220.

2. In *Lire Les Misérables*, pp. 119–134.

3. This work, which was premiered on 7 March 1843 at the Comédie Française, ran to only thirty-six performances and was the biggest box-office failure in Hugo's career. The audience laughed at some of the verses, the critics were sardonic, and he became the butt of comedians and cartoonists. After that, Victor Hugo never wrote another play.

4. Quoted in Guillemin, *Pierres*, p. 267.

5. It is not surprising, therefore, that *Les Misérables* is the novel that has been most adapted to the theater, to radio, and to the cinema, that there are so many children's adaptations, cartoons, or comic versions, and that it has inspired so many painters, cartoonists, and graphic artists.

6. All the quotations have been taken from Pedro Calderón de la Barca, *El gran teatro del mundo*, ed. and introd. John J. Allen and Domingo Ynduráin (Barcelona: Crítica, 1997).

7. Leuilliot, *Lire Les Misérables*, p. 73.

8. It is not certain that Cambronne ever uttered this *merde*. In his edition of *Les Misérables* (Paris: Bibliothèque de La Pléiade, Gallimard,

1951), pp. 1155–1156, Maurice Allem sums up the inconclusive debate surrounding the matter. According to some, the phrase in question was more declamatory: "The guard will die, but it will never surrender!" although Cambronne, who survived Waterloo, always denied ever having delivered this maxim. But, according to one of his fellow prisoners in England, Monsieur Boyer-Peyreleau, Cambronne admitted having answered the English officer with the famous swear word, at the same time as exposing his backside to him, and giving it an insolent slap.

9. According to Albouy, *La Création mythologique*, p. 86 n. 150, Victor Hugo took the notion of human excrement as a fertilizer from Pierre Leroux, the author of *La Grève de Samarez*, which expounds this idea.

10. M. Bakhtin, *La cultura popular en la Edad Media y en el Renacimiento* (Barcelona: Barral Editores, 1974).

11. In his excellent study of the novels of Victor Hugo, Victor Brombert points out that the author of *Les Misérables* "anticipated" the theories of Bakhtin on the grotesque and the carnivalesque. See *Victor Hugo and the Visionary Novel* (Cambridge, Mass.: Harvard University Press, 1984), p. 71.

12. Ubersfeld, in *Lire Les Misérables*, p. 126.

13. In a poem from *Les Feuilles d'automne*, entitled "La pente de la rêverie," in which the poet suddenly has a vision of the universe, Victor Hugo makes an enumeration that anticipates that famous enumeration of Borges in "El Aleph": "I saw the populous sea, I saw the dawn, and the evening . . .":

Alors, tours, aqueducs, pyramides, colonnes,
Je vis l'intérieur des vieilles Babylonnes,
Les Carthages, les Tyres, les Thébes, les Sions
D'où sans cesse sortaient les générations.
Ainsi j'embrassai tout: et la terre, et Cybelle,
La face antique après de la face nouvelle;
Le passé, le présent; les vivants et les morts;
Le genre humain complet comme au jour de remords . . .

CHAPTER V: *Rich, Poor, Leisured, Idle, and Marginal*

1. *Reliquat des Misérables*, Edition de l'Imprimerie National (Paris: Paul Ollendorf, 1908–1909), vols. 2–3, p. 554.

2. Victor Hugo, *Choses vues*, September 1848, *Histoire*, Laffont, p. 1091.

3. *Reliquat des Misérables*, vols. 2–3, p. 608.

4. The text is in *Reliquat des Misérables*, vol. 4, beginning p. 356.

5. *Reliquat des Misérables*, vol. 4, p. 347. In *Le Mythe du peuple dans Les Misérables* (Paris: Editions Sociales, 1964), p. 214, René Journet and Guy Robert quote another unpublished text by Hugo that talks about his political evolution, which they believe dates from 1849–1850 but seems later: "From the age that my spirit opened and I began to take part in the political transformations and social fluctuations of my time, my conscience has followed unswervingly the following phases in its journey to the light:

1818 realist
1824 liberal realist
1827 liberal
1828 liberal socialist
1830 democratic liberal socialist
1849 democratic liberal socialist republican

6. Aurevilly, *Les Misérables de M. V. Hugo*, p. 5.

7. *Le Mythe du peuple dans Les Misérables*, p. 136.

8. Gustave Flaubert, *Correspondance* (Paris: Louis Conard, 1929), vol. 5, p. 35.

9. M. A. de Lamartine, "Considérations sur un chef d'oeuvre, ou le danger du génie: *Les Misérables*, par Victor Hugo," in *Cours familier de Littérature. Un entretien par mois*, vol. 14 (Paris, 1862), pp. 305–432, and vol. 15 (Paris, 1863), pp. 5–224.

10. Gay, *Los Miserables de Victor Hugo*, pp. 34–35.

11. *Reliquat des Misérables*, final vol., pp. 362 ff.

12. *Reliquat des Misérables*, vols. 2 and 3, VI, p. 549.

13. *Reliquat des Misérables*, Vols 2 and 3, IV, p. 546.

14. Adèle Hugo, *Victor Hugo raconté par un témoin de sa vie* (Paris: Librairie International, 1863), vol. 1, p. 49.

15. Adèle Hugo, *Victor Hugo raconté par un témoin de sa vie*, vol. 2, chap. 51, pp. 165–168.

16. Patrice Boussel and Madelaine Dubois, *De quoi vivait Victor Hugo?* (Paris: Edition des Deux Rives, 1952), p. 66.

17. Jacques Robichon, *Le Roman d'un chef-d'oeuvre: Les Misérables* (Paris: Les Oeuvres Libres, Revue Mensuelle consacrée a l'inédit, Librairie Arthème Fayard, June 1959), pp. 97–142.

18. Jean Pommier, "Premier pas dans l'étude des Misérables," *Bulletin de la Faculté des Lettres de Strasbourg*, issue dedicated to Victor Hugo, no. 40, January–March 1961–1962, pp. 281–289.

19. Adèle Hugo, *Victor Hugo raconté par un témoin de sa vie*, vol. 1, pp. 264–266.

20. *Actes et paroles, Avant l'Exil*, in *Oeuvres Complètes*, vol. 7 (Paris: Club Français dur Livre, 1968), p. 119.

21. See the excellent anthology of texts by Hugo on this theme, *Ecrits de Victor Hugo sur la peine de mort*, ed. Raymond Jean (Avignon: Editions Actas/Sud, 1979).

22. Adèle Hugo, *Victor Hugo raconté par un témoin de sa vie*, vol. 2, pp. 225–244.

CHAPTER VI: *Civilized Barbarians*

1. He will also say of the Battle of Waterloo that it was "as obscure for the winners as for the loser" (II, I, XVI, p. 358).

2. Jean-Marc Hovasse, *Victor Hugo*, vol. 1, *Avant l'exil, 1802–1851* (Paris: Fayard, 2001), p. 539.

3. Adèle Hugo, *Victor Hugo raconté par un témoin de sa vie*, vol. 2, pp. 322–323.

4. Quoted in Hubert Juin, *Victor Hugo*, vol. 1 (Paris: Flammarion, 1980), p. 669.

5. See two articles that analyze what Victor Hugo saw, researched, and invented about the insurrection of 5 June 1832 and the sources he used: Emile Tersen, "Le Paris des *Misérables*," and Gérard Milhaud, "De l'histoire au roman," both published in the issue of *Europe* dedicated to the novel on its centenary (Paris: February–March, 1962); and Louis Blanc, *Histoire des Dix Ans*, vols. 1–4 (Brussels: Société Typographique Belge, 1850), a book that Victor Hugo also consulted.

6. *Le Code des gens honnêtes* (Paris, 1825).

7. Louis Chevalier, *Classes laborieuses et classes dangereuses à Paris pendant la première moitié du XIX siècle* (Paris: Plon, 1958), introduction, p. XV.

8. Chevalier argues that in *Les Misérables*, Hugo was the novelist who most faithfully reflected the "criminal" aspect of his age—more so than Balzac and Sue—because, he says, his was the first novel to show the *classes dangereuses* and the *classes laborieuses* not as rigorously separate, but as intimately linked, and to understand that crime was a "by-product" of poverty and that they both affected the whole of society. From this standpoint—the sociological view of crime that appears in the novel—Chevalier's statement has a certain weight. But, as he himself recognizes, it is in Hugo's "involuntary" account that he is most faithful to criminal reality, while his depiction of the bandits of the novel—the famous quartet from Patron-Minette who run nocturnal crime in Paris—was even

more conventional and homespun than the serial novels that came before him.

## CHAPTER VII: *From Heaven Above*

1. *Les Misérables*, ed. Marius-François Guyard (Paris: Classiques
Garnier, 1957).

2. The text was included in the Edition de L'Imprimerie Nationale
(Paris: Paul Ollendorf, 1908), pt. 1, vol. 3, pp. 309–400.

3. "La préface philosophique des *Misérables*," *Bulletin de la Faculté des
Lettres du Strasbourg*, January–March 1962, pp. 315–328.

## CHAPTER VIII: *The Temptation of the Impossible*

1. M. A. de Lamartine, "Considérations sur un chef-d'oeuvre, ou le
danger du génie: *Les Misérables* par Victor Hugo," in *Cours familier de
Littérature. Un entretien par mois*, vol. 14 (Paris, 1862), pp. 305–432, and
vol. 15 (Paris, 1863), pp. 5–224.

2. Lamartine was centrally involved in the Revolution.

3. "From the point of view of the genuinely conservative institution the ideal is obedience, not enthusiasm, whatever the nature of the
enthusiasm. Not for nothing was 'Ruhe ist die erste Buergerpflicht'
(Tranquility is the first duty of the citizen) the slogan of every German
princeling." E. J. Hobsbawm, *Primitive Rebels*, 3rd ed. (Manchester:
Manchester University Press, 1978), p. 119.

# Index

Note: "LM" refers to Les Misérables, and "VH" refers to Victor Hugo. Following the style of the text, many of the characters are indexed by their first names, for example, Cosette and Gavroche.

ABC conspirators, 118
the absolute, 153
Académie Française, 171–72
active craters. See craters
"affaire Champmathieu," 19, 102–3, 123, 124, 162–63
"A la jeune France" (VH), 140
Albouy, Pierre, 83, 154–55, 181n.9
"El Aleph" (Borges), 104, 181n.13
Allem, Maurice, 181n.8
Angelin, Canon, 127–28
Angers, David d', 127
assault, 143
atheism/skepticism, 149, 150, 151, 153, 156
Athélie ou les Scandinaves (VH), 2
authoritarian power's paranoia, 174–75
Azelma (character), 83, 91

Babet (character), 68, 85–86, 89
Bahorel (character), 85
Bakhtin, Mikhail, 100–101
Balzac, Honoré de, 8–9, 27, 142–43, 158–59; La Comédie humaine, 65; Les Illusions perdues, 65–66
Bamatabois (character), 121, 123

banned books, 140, 170, 174
barbarism vs. culture/civilization, 113, 137, 177
Barbès, Armand, 129
Barbey D'Aurevilly, Jules Amédée, 43, 109, 165, 179n.1 (ch. 2)
barricade at La Chanvrerie. See La Chanvrerie barricade
Bataille, Georges, 77–78
Baudelaire, Charles, 33
Berry, Charles Ferdinand, duc de, 126
Bienvenu, Monseigneur. See Myriel, Bienvenu
Blachevelle (character), 84–85
Blanqui, Louis Auguste, 129
Blücher, General (character), 135
body vs. soul of characters, 49
bohemian students (characters), 84–85, 118, 120, 168
Bonapartists, 141
Borges, Jorge Luis: "El Aleph," 104, 181n.13
Bossuet (character), 71
Boyer-Peyreleau, M., 181n.8
Breton, André, 9
Brevet (character), 86

Brombert, Victor, 181n.11
Brown, John, 129
Bruneseau, Inspector General, 100
*Bug-Jargal* (VH), 79
*Les Burgraves* (VH), 88, 180n.3 (ch. 4)

Calderón de la Barca, Pedro: *El gran teatro del mundo*, 92–94
Cambronne, Pierre Jacques Étienne, 97–98, 135, 180–81n.8
Camus, Albert, 105–6; *L'Étranger*, 76
Carlists, 141
Catholic Church, 63, 72, 174
Cavaignac, General, 172
censorship, 174–75
Cervantes, Miguel de: *Don Quixote*, 10, 174
Champmathieu, M., 19, 102–3, 119, 123, 124, 162–63
chance: and coincidence, order of, 40, 43, 46; and destiny, 34–41; and pre-determination of history, 38, 54; role of in plot development, 38–40, 43–44, 46, 47–48; and whims, 40. *See also* coincidence
characters, 56–86; abstract/anony-mous, 45; abundance of, 34–35; angels with dirty faces, 80–82 (*see also* Éponine; Gavroche); as arche-typal/immoderate, 56–57; body vs. soul of, 49; chaste, 70–75; collec-tive, 84–86; conflicts within, 48–49; vs. destiny, 51; employment of, 118–20; the fanatic, 75–80 (*see also* Javert); and feelings of insignifi-cance, 54–55; freedom vs. fate of, 52–54; good/bad (monsters), 57–58, 60, 61, 69, 82–83; and identity, 55; instinctive behavior of, 60–61; the just man, 65–70 (*see also* Val-jean, Jean); meetings of in sewers of Paris, 47–48, 158; monologues/dia-logues of, 19–21, 94; motivations of, 45–46; name changes/identities of, 87–88, 102–3; and Napoleon

figures, 54; number of, 84; reli-gious, 120; the saint, 61–65 (*see also* Myriel, Bienvenu); social injustices fought by, 114–17; subordination of to narrator, 92, 93–94; theatrical-ity of, 89, 90–92, 94, 133–34. *See also specific characters*
Charles X, King, 140
chastity, 70–75
Chateaubriand, François-Auguste-René, vicomte de, 168
Chenildieu (character), 86
Chevalier, Louis, 142–43, 183–84n.8
children, abandoned, 143
cholera, 143
civilization, progress of, 136, 177
Claquesous (character), 68, 85–86, 89
*Claude Gueux* (VH), 27, 127
Cochepaille (character), 86
Cocteau, Jean, 9
coincidence, 39–48; and fate, 41, 45; order of, 39–41, 43, 46; and premo-nitions, 43–44; role of in plot devel-opment, 41, 42, 43–44, 46, 47–48. *See also* chance
Colegio de los Nobles (Madrid), 6–7
Combeferre (character), 19–20, 85, 133
*La Comédie humaine* (Balzac), 65
communists' paranoia regarding fic-tion, 174
La Conciergerie, 128
consequences, 38
constiutionalism, 141
consumers vs. producers, 120, 167
Convention, 110
Cosette (character): bedroom of, 17; chain gang met by, 128; chastity of, 71, 72–73; and courtship of Marius, 169; love of for Marius, 38, 73; Marius falls in love with, 60; mar-riage of to Marius, 14; name changes of, 91; Order of Perpetual Adoration's sheltering of, 12; role changes of, 91; Mme Thénardier's cruelty toward, 83; Valjean leaves,

69, 70; Valjean's love for, 67; Valjean's rescue of, 96; Valjean's self-sacrifice for, 46; wedding of, 73
coup of 1851, 107
Courfeyrac (character), 37, 85
craters: and destiny, 51; La Chanvrerie barricade, 47; in *LM*, 21–22, 42–43, 47; in the narrative, 45; in novels generally, 41–42; and plot movement, 45; sewers of Paris, 47
crime serial novels, 143, 183–84n.8
criminals, 142–44, 183–84n.8
criticism. *See* Lamartine, Alphonse de, critique of *LM*; *Les Misérables*, reception of
*Cromwell* (VH), 8–9
culture/civilization vs. barbarism, 113, 137, 177

Dahlia (character), 84–85
Daix, 129
death penalty, 109, 124–30
deaths, theatricality of, 95
*Le Déluge* (VH), 2
democracy, 151, 152–53, 155
*Le Dernier Jour d'un condamné* (VH), 27, 127–28, 129
Deschamps, Émile, 139
destiny, 34–55; vs. characters, 51; and craters, 51; vs. human agency, 37–38; and law of chance/order of coincidence, 34–41; and revolution, 133, 135–36, 138; and social injustice, 105–6, 122
destitution, 109
dialogues vs. monologues, 18–19, 94
Dickens, Charles, 8–9
dictatorships' paranoia regarding fiction, 174–75
Digne, Miollis de, 28
divine predetermination, 133. *See also* destiny; fate
*Don Quixote* (Cervantes), 10, 174
Drouet, Juliette, 3, 8, 73, 74–75, 128
Dumas, Alexandre: *The Three Musketeers*, 80

education/knowledge as cure for social injustice, 109–10, 116, 122
*L'Éducation Sentimentale* (Flaubert), 113
egalitarian socialism, 116
Elephant of the Bastille, 81, 97
employment, 118–20
Enjolras (character): chastity of, 70–71; choices of, 54; and companions, 85; death of, 12–13, 85, 95; fanaticism of, 77; Javert interrogated by, 76–77; motivations of, 45; his vision of future society, 111–12, 114, 132–33
enthusiasm as subversive, 171, 175–76, 184n.3 (ch. 8)
Entrails of the Leviathan. *See* sewers of Paris
"Epic of the Rue Saint-Denis" (VH), 131–32, 133–34, 138, 139, 141–42, 169. *See also* Paris uprising
Éponine (character): as a good character, 57–58, 83; injustice toward vs. fate of, 106; love of for Marius, 83, 106; name changes of, 91; saintly character of, 61–62; spectral quality of, 83–84
*L'Étranger* (Camus), 76
executions, sadistic crowds at, 125, 127

Fabantou (character; *pseud.* M. Thénardier). *See* Thénardier, M.
Fabre, Urbain (character; *pseud.* Jean Valjean), 87. *See also* Valjean, Jean
factory workers, 119
faith in God, 152, 154, 156
Fameuil (character), 84–85
Fantine (character), 118–19; background/sufferings of, 72, 121; death of, 76, 95; detained by Javert, 121; fired for being a single mother, 116; name changes of, 91; prostitution of, 121; ruined by Thénardier, 71; and seamstress companions, 84–85

fascists' paranoia regarding fiction, 174

fate: and coincidence, 41, 45; vs. freedom, 52–53; and God, 53–54; as a plot device, 45; and revolution, 133, 135–36, 138; and social injustice, 105–6, 122

Fauchelevent, Ultime (character; *pseud.* Jean Valjean), 36–37, 87. *See also* Valjean, Jean

Faulkner, William, 174

Favourite (character), 84–85

*feuilleton*, romantic, 35

Feuilly (character), 85

fiction. *See* novels

Flaubert, Gustave, 30–31; *L'Éducation Sentimentale*, 113; on *LM*, 115–16; *Madame Bovary*, 30, 113, 164; narrators used by, 31, 164; religious skepticism of, 164

Fourier, François-Marie-Charles, 166

freedom, 52–55, 151–52

French Revolution (1789–1795), 110, 111, 136–37

*Les Fumeaux* (VH), 88

G (character; Conventionist): death of, 95; goodness of, 111; and Myriel, 111, 167; as an outcast, 110; politics of, 110, 111, 114; romanticism of, 110; "strange light" emanating from, 111

Gavroche (character): appeal of, 80–81, 82; character traits of, 80–81; as comic character, 20; death of, 82, 95; in the Elephant of the Bastille, 81, 97; as a good character, 57–58, 59, 81–82; injustice toward vs. fate of, 106; motivations of, 45–46; recognizes Javert at the barricades, 76; saintly character of, 61–62, 67; theatricality of, 89; unruliness/marginality represented by, 81–82

Gay, Narciso, 33, 108–9, 116

Genflot (character; *pseud.* M. Thénardier). *See* Thénardier, M.

Gillenormand, M. (character), 20–21, 58–60, 94, 118

Girardin, Delphine de, 4

God: Battle of Waterloo decided by, 133–34; as a character in *LM*, 45; and democracy, 155; evil created/allowed by, 153; faith in, 152, 154, 156; and fate, 53–54; as first cause, 150; as the ideal, 147; infinite perspective of, 161; moral redemption/reconciliation with, 38; Nerval on existence of, 26–27; presence of, 145, 156; proof of existence of, 149–50, 153–54, 155–56; and republicanism, 152–53; vs. society as source of suffering, 168; the spiritual as dominant reality for, 162–63

Gorbeau tenement, 43–45, 97

Gosselin, Charles, 127

gothic stories, 97

Grand Guignol, 97

Grantaire (character), 20, 85, 95

*El gran teatro del mundo* (Calderón de la Barca), 92–94

Guelemer (character), 85–86. 89

Gueux, Claude, 129

Guillemin, Henri, 18, 70; *Hugo et la sexualité*, 8, 74

guillotine, 124–25, 127

Guyard, Marius-François, 48–49, 146

Habibrah (character), 79

harmony/solidarity, 151

*Hernani* (VH), 5, 27

historical optimism, 106, 111–12

history: all-encompassing, novel as, 158–59; as a character in *LM*, 45; as continuous progress, 137; vs. metaphysics, 105–6; as providential design, 133–34; shaping of, 54, 179–80n.4 (ch. 2)

Hobsbawm, Eric, 171, 184n.3 (ch. 8)

Hovasse, Jean-Marc, 1–2

Hugo, Adèle (*née* Foucher; VH's wife), 4; *Journal d'exil*, 63–64; marriage of to Victor, 3, 8, 73, 74–75;

and Sainte-Beuve, 74; on VH's wit-
nessing/knowledge of executions,
125, 126, 127; *Victor Hugo raconté
par un témoin de sa vie*, 125, 126,
139
Hugo, Charles (VH's son), 63–64,
125, 129
Hugo, Joseph Léopold Sigisbert
(VH's father), 6, 126
Hugo, Victor: in the Académie Française, 171–72; and adversity, 50–
51; Bakhtin anticipated by, 181n.11;
banned works of, 140, 174; on Bienvenu character, 63–64; childhood/
youth of, 6–7, 73–74, 125–26;
death/funeral of, 6; death penalty
opposed by, 125–30; executions wit-
nessed by, 125–27; in exile, 4, 6, 8,
75; exile's effects on, 51, 107–8;
and fate, views on, 50–51; finances
of, 7, 75; as French romantic, 2; ge-
nius of, 8–9; influence/fame of,
5–6, 9; and Juliette, 3, 8, 73, 74–
75, 128; Lamartine's relationship
with, 171–72; on length of *LM*, 22;
his love of life, 3; in Madrid, 6–7;
marriage of to Adèle, 3, 8, 73, 74–
75; notebooks kept by, 7–8, 179n.1
(introduction); and the Paris uprising (1832), 26, 138–45; personality
of, 9; and philosophies of freedom,
51; as poet, 5, 6; politics of, 12–13,
107–9, 140–41, 155, 182n.5; popularity of, 5–6; precociousness of, 2;
prisoners/prison life observed by,
127–29; prison system criticized by,
128–29; religious leanings/practices
of, 3–4, 64, 154, 164 (*see also* "Philosophical Preface"); return of to
France, 6; séances conducted by,
4–5; sexual exploits of, 3, 8, 74–75,
179n.1 (introduction); Spanish influence on, 6–7; spiritual enrichment as a goal of his writings, 9–
10; on virginity at marriage, 73;
volume of writings by and on, 1–3.

**Works:** "A la jeune France," 140;
*Athélie ou les Scandinaves*, 2; *Bug-
Jargal*, 79; *Les Burgraves*, 88, 180n.3
(ch. 4); *Claude Gueux*, 27, 127;
*Cromwell*, 8–9; *Le Déluge*, 2; *Le Dernier Jour d'un condamné*, 27, 127–
28, 129; *Les Fumeaux*, 88; *Hernani*,
5, 27; "L'Hymne aux morts de juillet," 140; *Inez de Castro*, 2; *Marion
de Lorme*, 140; *Les Misères*, 21; *Notre-Dame de Paris*, 5, 8–9; "La
pente de la rêverie," 181n.13; "Philosophie, commencement d'un livre," 64; *Le Roi s'amuse*, 139
*Hugo et la sexualité* (Guillemin), 8, 74
human excrement as fertilizer, 28, 99,
158, 181n.9
humanity, theme of, 50
"L'Hymne aux morts de juillet" (VH),
140

Idea (abstract being), 4–5
idle people, 118, 119–20
ignorance/prejudices, 109, 111,
121–22
*Les Illusions perdues* (Balzac), 65–66
Index of banned books, 174
*Inez de Castro* (VH), 2
infanticide, 143
the infinite, 148–54
information, hiding/supression of, 16
injustices. *See* social injustices/ills
intuition, 151
invisible hand metaphor, 52
irresistible traps. *See* craters

Jacobin Terror, 167
Javert (character): authority/law respected by, 76; background of, 76;
as a bad character, 57–58, 59, 75–
76; captured/condemned to death,
76–77, 78; chastity of, 70–71; civili-
zation/reason represented by, 77–
78, 81; courage of, 76–77, 78;
doubts/confusion of, 78–80; employment of, 118, 120; fanaticism

Javert (character) (*cont.*)
of, 77; Fantine detained by, 121; and La Chanvrerie barricade, 46–47; Madeleine suspected by, 60–61, 78; motivations of, 45; rebellion hated by, 76; strength of, 71; suicide of, 79–80, 95; theatricality of, 90–91; and Valjean, 46, 49–50, 68, 76, 78, 80

Joly (character), 85

Jondrette (character; *pseud.* M. Thénardier), 68, 85–86, 90. *See also* Thénardier, M.

*Journal d'exil* (A. Hugo), 63–64

Journet, René, 115, 118, 182n.5

judicial/prison system, injustices of, 109, 118, 122–24, 130

July Monarchy. *See* Louis Philippe, King

July Revolution (Paris, 1848), 172, 173

junkmen's revolt (1832), 144

Kerles, Hamet de, 155

La Chanvrerie barricade: consequences of, 46; as a crater, 47; and Javert, 46–47; meeting of protagonists in, 45–46; setting related to actions at, 101; and Valjean, 46–47. *See also* Paris uprising; rebels; revolution

Lahorie, General, 126

Laigle (or Lesgle; character), 85

Lamarque, Maximilien, 65, 139, 141

Lamartine, Alphonse de: involvement of in the Revolution, 166, 184n.2 (ch. 8); political career of, 172, 173; VH's relationship with, 171–72

Lamartine, Alphonse de, critique of *LM*: on the bohemian students, 168; on characters as prisoners or deserving of prison, 116, 118, 166; as dangerous, 170–71, 172–73; on egalitarian socialism, 116; on the

"Epic of the Rue Saint-Denis," 169; on exaggerations/inaccuracies, 165–66, 167, 169–70; on fictional elements, 169; on fiction's function in history, 165, 166–67; on ideological lack of definition, 166; as the impossible, 166, 170; on "In the Year 1817" as treasonable, 168; on justification of crime, 167; on lack of realism, 168–71; as limitless progress, 170; as making people upset at being people, not God, 160, 167; on Marius and Cosette's courtship, 169; on Myriel's conversation with G, 167; on society vs. God as source of suffering, 168; sociopolitical condemnation of the genre, 170–71; on taxes/consumption, 167; on the title, 166; on use of *merde*, 168–69; as utopian novel, 166; on wordiness, 169

law as a source of social injustice, 122–24, 130

Leblanc, M. (character; *pseud.* Jean Valjean), 87, 97. *See also* Valjean, Jean

Lefèvre, Jules, 126–27

legitimists, 141

Leray, Anatole, 153

Lesclide, Juana Richard, 74

Lesgle (or Laigle; character), 85

Leuilliot, Bernard, 95

liberalism, 141

liberation theology, 63

light/shadow, 95–96

Listolier (character), 84–85

literature, 57, 61, 173–74, 175. *See also* novels

"Long Live Death!" slogan, 134

Louis Bonaparte, 107

Louis Philippe, King (July Monarchy), 129, 140, 141, 144–45, 172

Louis XVI, King, 110

Louvel, Louis Pierre, 126

Mabeuf, M. (character): death of, 92; as a good character, 57–58; poverty of, 122; as rentier, 118; role changes of, 91–92

Mabuse, M. (character), 95, 101–2

*Madame Bovary* (Flaubert), 30, 113, 164

Madeleine, M. (character; *pseud.* Jean Valjean): as the good rich man, 114–15; invention/prosperity of, 114–15; Javert's suspicions of, 60–61, 78; model for, 65; philanthropy of, 115; on poverty, 115; Valjean's transformation into, 87. *See also* Valjean, Jean

Maistre, Joseph de, 167

man as holding power of life/death over inferior creatures, 150–51

Manichaean vision, 61

*Marion de Lorme* (VH), 140

Marius (character): in ABC group, 61; chastity of, 71, 72–73; Cosette falls in love with, 60; his courtship of Cosette, 169; employment of, 118; on Éponine and Azelma, 83; Gillenormand's treatment by, 58–60; on the La Chanvrerie barricade, 58–59; his love for Cosette, 38, 73; his marriage to Cosette, 14; and Meux, 37; motivations of, 45; normality of, 58–60; political ideas of, 12–13, 108; role changes of, 91; on Valjean's character traits, 65; Valjean's rescue of, 46, 99; Valjean's self-sacrifice for, 46; Valjean's treatment by, 58, 60; wedding of, 73

Martin, Jean, 126–27

Marx, Karl, 179–80n.4 (ch. 2)

Maurin, Pierre, 28, 127–28

Maurois, André, 61

Meaux, Laigle de (character), 37

media, propaganda via, 175

medieval literature, 57, 61

Melville, Herman, 8–9

*Merde!*, 98–99, 168–69, 180–81n.8

metaphysics vs. history, 105–6

*Les Misérables* (VH): active volcanic craters in, 21–22, 42–43, 47; ambitiousness of, 8–9; burned by Spanish bishops, 109; as a children's novel, 32–33; classical vs. modern moments in, 47; conventions of, 18, 21, 32; the divine in, 9–10; epigraph of, 106–7, 146–47; episodes of deemed unbelievable, 116; evolution of/revisions to, 12–13; force/memorableness of, 13; freedom of characters in, 32; goals of, 106–7, 147, 154, 155, 173 (*see also* social injustices/ills); good/bad actions in, 161–63; vs. *El gran teatro del mundo*, 92–94; the impossible attempted by, 155–56; influence of, 176–77; length of, 22; makeup of, 41; Manichaean vision of, 61; Marxist perspective on, 115; vs. *Les Misères*, 12–13; morality of, 72, 74–75; pace of, 21–22, 23–24; political views in, changes in, 108–9; quality of, 23; reality/truth vs. fiction in, 19–20, 23–29, 33, 40, 113–14, 117; reception of, 32–33, 98, 108–9, 111, 115–17, 180n.2 (ch. 3) (*see also* Lamartine, Alphonse de, critique of *LM*); as a religious tract, 4, 64, 164; rhetorical level of, 21; romanticism of, 57; significant events in, 41; slang in, 127; sources for, 90; subversiveness of, 108–9; totality/deicidal impulse manifested in, 22, 156–64, 173. *See also* "Philosophical Preface"

*Les Misérables de M. V. Hugo* (Barbey D'Aurevilly), 179n.1 (ch. 2)

*Les Misères* (VH), 12–13, 21

misfortune, theme of, 46

monarchy, 152–53, 156

monologues, 18–19, 20–21, 94

Montparnasse (character), 68, 85–86

Montreuil-sur-mer, 162–63

moralists on self-punishment, 69
morality, legal prejudices concerning, 123
Myriel, Bienvenu (character): accompanies condemned man to guillotine, 125; charity of, 114; and G, 111, 167; as a good character, 57–58, 59; house of, 102; model for, 28, 127–28; saintly character of, 61–64, 67, 180n.2 (ch. 3); social philosophy of, 114; and Valjean's spiritual conversion, 64–65, 66
*Les Mystères de Paris* (Sue), 90

name changes/identities of characters, 87–88, 102–3
Napoleon Bonaparte, 98, 107, 134, 136
narrator of *LM*, 11–33; as all-powerful, 15; on Cambronne, 97–98; on chance, 35, 38; characteristics of, 12, 16–17; characters' subordination to, 92, 93–94; contradictions of, 17–18; conventions established by, 18–19; on destiny, 34; doubts/silences/ignorance of, 15–16; euphonic repetition by, 17; excessiveness of, 13; on excrement of sewers, 99–100; on history vs. fate, 105; vs. Hugo, 11, 26–29; on human excrement as fertilizer, 28, 99; on injustices and fate, 106; on law, 76; as main character, 11; narcissism of, 14; narrative slowness of, 23–25; as nonintegral character, 22; omniscience of, 12, 14–15, 16; optimistic vision of, 36; on order/progress of events, 35–36; precision of, 14; on religion, 25; on revolution, 132, 135, 136–38, 145; as stenographer, 15; totalizing/deicidal vision of, 158–61, 163–64; unconsciousness of, 31–32; on Waterloo, 97–98, 136, 183n.1
narrators of novels, generally, 22, 29–31
national guard, 86

Nerval, Gérard de, 26–27
Ney (character), 135
*Notre-Dame de Paris* (VH), 5, 8–9
novels: banned, 140, 170, 174; classical vs. modern, 30–33; as entertainment/amusement, 173–74; impetus for fictions, 173; irresistible traps in, 41–43; life in, vs. real life, 103–4, 117; narrative structure of, 42; narrators in, 22 (*see also* narrators of novels, generally); organizational structure of, 42; readers' enrichment by, 9–10; as subversive, 170–71, 172–76; as taking readers to impossible worlds, 171, 173, 175–76; technique/style of, 42; unease created by, 175–76
nuns, 86, 120

ontological pessimism, 106
Order of Perpetual Adoration, 12, 158
original sin and redemption, 69
Owen, Robert, 114

Paris uprising (1832): "Epic of the Rue Saint-Denis," 131–32, 133–34, 138, 139, 141–42, 144–45; fear/terror/crime preceding, 143–44; historical vs. fictional account of, 131–32, 142, 144–45, 183–84n.8; Lemarque funeral as spark for, 65, 144; stamped out by national guard, 86; and VH, 26, 138–45. *See also* La Chanvrerie barricade
Paris uprising (July Revolution; 1848), 172, 173
Patron-Minette gang (characters), 68, 85–86, 89, 127, 183–84n.8
"La pente de la rêverie" (VH), 181n.13
Petit Picpus, 86, 101, 158
"Philosophical Preface" (VH), 146–64; on the absolute, 153; on atheism/skepticism, 149, 150, 151, 153, 156; on democracy, 151, 152–53, 155; on the earth and objects in

space, 148–49; on faith in God, 152, 154, 156; on fiction and the real world, 147; on freedom/responsibility, 151–52; on God, and democracy, 155; on God, proof of existence of, 149–50, 153–54, 155–56; on God as the ideal, 147; on harmony/solidarity, 151; the impossible attempted by, 155–56; on the infinite, 148–54; interpretation of, 154–55; on intuition, 151; vs. *LM*, 155–56; on man as holding power of life/death over inferior creatures, 150–51; metaphysical observations in, 148–49; on misfortune's sources, 154; on monarchy, 152–53, 156; on poverty, 154; on prayer, 154, 156; on religions/superstition, 150, 153, 156; on scientific progress, 152; on the soul, and democracy, 155; on the soul, proof of existence of, 147, 150–54; transcendent life, goal of demonstrating, 147; VH begins writing, 146
"Philosophie, commencement d'un livre" (VH), 64
Pierre, Abbé, 63
plague, 143, 144
Plato: *Republic*, 166
plot: active volcanic craters in, 45; chance's role in developing, 38–40, 43–44, 46, 47–48; coincidence's role in developing, 41, 42, 43–44, 46, 47–48; crossroads in, 44; fate's role in developing, 45, 51, 52–54; meetings of characters in, 40, 46, 47–48, 49–50; and mystery, 48; political dimension of, 46; structure of, 48; subjective vs. objective views of humanity in, 50; whims of characters in, 40
Pommier, Jean, 128
Ponine (character; *pseud.* Éponine), 91. See also Éponine
Pontmarin, Armand de, 128
Pontmercy, Colonel, 158, 161–62

poverty, 50, 109, 115, 122, 143, 154, 183–84n.8
prayer, 154, 156
"Préface Philosophique." See "Philosophical Preface"
prejudices/ignorance, 109, 111, 121–22
premonitions, 43–44
priests, 120
prison system. See judicial/prison system, injustices of
producers vs. consumers, 120, 167
progress: of civilization, 136, 177; faith in, 112; history as, 137; limitless, 170; and revolution, 133, 135–38; scientific, 152
propaganda, 175
prostitution, 118, 121–22, 142–43
Proudhon, P. J., 33
Prouvaire, Jean (character), 85
providence, 48

rebels (characters), 118, 120; death of, 82, 134; desires/goals of, 141; and history as providential design, 133–34. See also revolution
reformist idealism, 110–14
relative values, 162–63
religions/superstition, 150, 153, 156
religious fundamentalists' paranoia regarding fiction, 174
rentiers, 118, 119–20
Republic, 141
*Republic* (Plato), 166
republicanism, 141, 152–53
responsibility/freedom, 151–52
Résséguier, Jules de, 139
Restoration, 140, 141
revolution, 131–45; and Enjolras's vision of future society, 132–33; and fate/destiny, 133, 135–36, 138; and history as providential design, 133–34; "Long Live Death!" slogan of, 134; narrator on, 132, 135, 136–38, 145; and progress, 133, 135–38. See also Paris uprising; Waterloo, Battle of

revolutionary students (characters), 85. *See also specific characters*
rich vs. poor, 120
robbery, 118, 120, 122, 143
Robert, Guy, 115, 118, 182n.5
Robichon, Jacques, 128
*Le Roi s'amuse* (VH), 139
romanticism: and Manichaean vision, 61; *maudit* aspects of behavior recognized by, 77–78; Spanish, 6; VH's, 2
Rousseau, Jean-Jacques: *Social Contract*, 166
Rue de La Chanvrerie. *See* La Chanvrerie barricade
Rue Plumet garden, 101–2, 159–60

Sainte-Beuve, Charles Augustin, 74, 140–41
Sainte-Pélagie prison riot (1832), 144
Saint-Simon, Claude Henri de Rouvroy, comte de, 112, 153, 166
Satan's redemption, 164
Schelicher, Victor, 155
scientific progress, 112, 113, 152
seamstresses (characters), 84–85, 119
settings, 96–97
sewers of Paris ("Entrails of the Leviathan"), 47–52; as a crater, 47; and meetings of characters, 47–48, 158; as setting, 99–101
sex, 71–72, 74, 123
Shakespeare, William, 2, 174
Simon, Gustave, 128
Sisters of Charity, 120
skepticism. *See* atheism/skepticism
slang, 127
*Social Contract* (Rousseau), 166
social injustices/ills, 105–30; acceptance of, 105–6; characters fighting against, 114–17; Christian spirit as cure for, 109; and consumers vs. producers, 120; criticism of *LM*'s depiction of, 115–16; death penalty, 109, 124–30; destitution, 109;

education/knowledge as cure for, 109–10, 116, 122; and employment, 118–20; and faith in progress, 112; and fate/destiny, 105–6, 122; in first vs. second version of *LM*, 108; historical optimism about, 106, 111–12; ignorance/prejudices, 109, 111, 121–22; of the judicial/prison system, 109, 118, 122–24, 130; law as a source of, 122–24, 130; literature's fight against, 106–9; ontological pessimism about, 106; poverty, 109, 115, 122; prostitution, 118, 121–22; and reformist idealism, 110–14; and rich vs. poor, 120; robbery, 118, 120, 122; scientific progress as cure for, 112, 113; and utopian vision vs. reality, 111–13; women, abuses suffered by, 120–22
socialist philosophy, 166
society vs. God as source of suffering, 168
Socrates, 95
soldiers at Waterloo, 86
solidarity/harmony, 151
soul: vs. body, of characters, 49; communication through souls, 151; and democracy, 155; latent vs. patent, 152; proof of existence of, 147, 150–54
Spanish Inquisition, 170, 174
Spanish romanticism, 6
Sue, Eugène, 27; *Les Mystères de Paris*, 90
suffering, as a character in *LM*, 45
suicide, 143
supernaturalism, 152
superstition/religions, 150, 153, 156

taxes, 167
Teresa, Mother, 63
theatricality, 87–104; adaptations of *LM*, 180n.5 (ch. 4); adjectives describing *LM*, 89–92; "affaire Champmathieu," 102–3; of Battle

of Waterloo, 134–35, 136; of characters, 89, 90–92, 94, 133–34; characters' subordination to narrator, 92, 93–94; deaths, 95; excess/exaggeration, 94–95; language/dialogues, 94; life as fiction, 102–4; light/shadow, 95–96; *Merde!*, 98–99, 180–81n.8; name changes/identities of characters, 87–88, 102–3; and plays by VH, 88–89; settings, 96–97; of situations, 133–34; Valjean's burning of his arm, 97
themes, 46, 50
Thénardier, M. (character), 61; adjectives describing, 90; ambushes Valjean, 68, 85–86; as a bad character, 57–58, 59, 82–83; cruelty of, 96; Fantine ruined by, 71; name changes of, 90; nature of, 49; Pontmercy rescued by, 158, 161–62; in sewers, 99; tavern run by, 101; at Waterloo, 103. *See also* Jondrette
Thénardier, Mme (character), 83, 91, 96
thieves, 118, 120, 122, 142–43
Tholomyès, Félix (character), 84–85, 121
*The Three Musketeers* (Dumas), 80
Tolstoy, Leo, 8–9; on *LM*, 33; *War and Peace*, 33, 174
totality/deicidal impulse, 22, 156–64, 173
Toulon prison, 128
Trébuchet, Sophie (VH's mother), 6–7, 107

Ubersfeld, Anne, 88, 89, 104
unemployment, 143
utopian vision vs. reality, 111–13

Valjean, Jean (character): and the "affaire Champmathieu," 19, 102–3, 123, 124, 162–63; agility of, 65; ambushed at Gorbeau tenement, 68, 85–86; bad side of, 66; burns his own arm, 68, 97; candlesticks beside deathbed of, 64–65; chain gang met by, 128; character traits of, 65; chastity of, 70–71; confession to Marius of his escape from galleys, 19; Cosette rescued by, 96; death of, 12, 95; duty/ obedience to law by, 69–70; his escape attempts from galleys, 66; his escape from Montreuil-sur-mer, 15–16; excessive humanity of, 65, 67–68; and Fauchelevent, 37; as a good character, 57–58, 59, 61–62, 65–66; injustice toward vs. fate of, 106; intelligence/knowledge of, 67; and Javert, 46, 49–50, 68, 76, 78, 80; and La Chanvrerie barricade, 46–47; leaves Cosette, 69, 70; love between Marius and Cosette sensed by, 61; his love for Cosette, 67; as Madeleine (*see* Madeleine, M.); Marius saved by, 46, 99; Marius's treatment of, 58, 60; masochism/suffering of, 67, 68–70; model for, 28, 127–28; monologues of, 20; motivations of, 45; and Myriel, 64–65, 66, 124; name changes of, 87–88; nature of, 49; Order of Perpetual Adoration's sheltering of, 12; his penance/redemption in the sewers, 101; prisoners with, 86; prison's transformation of, 124; religious leanings of, 69; as rentier, 118; his self-sacrifice for Cosette and Marius's happiness, 46; sentenced for stealing loaf of bread, 66, 116; spiritual purification of, 36, 64–67; strength of, 65, 71; terror felt by, 123
Vaquerie, Auguste, 155
Vautrin (character), 65–66
Veuillot, Louis, 117
*Victor Hugo raconté par un témoin de sa vie* (A. Hugo), 125, 126, 139
Victurnien, Mme (character), 118–19
volcanic craters. *See* craters
Voltaire, 169